What's In a Name?

Explaining Biblical Names

Bob Bedford

A Bedford Press Publication

Copyright © 2012 by Bob Bedford

What's In a Name?

ISBN #978-0-9848117-1-7

All rights reserved. No part of this publication may be reproduced or transmitted in any form or by any means without written permission of the author.

Unless otherwise noted Scripture is taken from the NEW AMERICAN STANDARD BIBLE @ 1960, 1962, 1963, 1968, 1971, 1972, 1973, 1975, 1977, by The Lockman Foundation. Used by permission.

Printed in the United States of America

Forewords

Most of us have one name, given at birth, which we keep for life. It is very personal, it is who we are, a sound that identifies us and that we respond to. As a young man in sales work I learned the power of a person's name as I was taught that "a person's name is the sweetest name in the English language".

God established the importance of a name when He named Himself in Exodus 3:14. Then in verse 15 He expanded on it: "....this is my name forever, and this is my memorial unto all generations." God further established the importance of a name as He deliberately changed the names of Abraham (Abram), Sarah (Sara), Israel (Jacob) and Peter (Simon), thereby changing their identity and memorializing their accomplishments and spiritual potential. He has also promised that all of us who have accepted Jesus Christ as our Savior and are following Him obediently will receive a new name in heaven. (Rev. 2:17)

As I read through this short story series addressing 'What's in a name', I looked forward to learning about each new name, wondering how many more of these biblical names could be so significant. Dr. Bedford has interestingly and skillfully observed names of Bible characters with the stories relating to them, coupled that with modern day analogies, and from that extracted practical applications for our everyday spiritual walk. I know that your Christian walk will be enriched, just as mine has, by the reading and rereading of these insights straight from God's Word.

--Pastor Jeff Yount
Mifflinburg PA

What's in a name? I can remember, as a young child, my parents telling me and my six siblings how important a name was. It was a statement of who we are. It could affect how we acted or how we would be treated. They told us that we became the name and the name became us. As wise GODly parents, they explained to us how important it was to have a "good name" which was more desirable than great riches and worth more than silver or gold. (Proverbs 22:1). GOD has used this truth about names to bless me and my family.

What's in a name? This seemingly insignificant question has an impact so huge that in answer to Moses' question GOD stated his name as "I AM WHO I AM". GOD instructed Moses to tell the Israelites that "I AM sent you". (Exodus 3:14). *What's in a name?* HE has given the name above all names, "JESUS", to HIS SON our LORD and SAVIOR. How can a name be above all other names unless GOD, the Creator and the Name-giver, gives everyone else a name below the name of JESUS? Almighty GOD created us, male and female, in HIS image. When someone asks us "who are you?" we respond, "I am (a reference to the image of GOD) my name (who I am)".

What's in a name? is a most fascinating and readable book.. As I was reading these *What's in a name?* devotional essays, I was impressed with the depth of insight that my good friend, Dr. Bob Bedford had into the concept of a name. My encouragement to him to publish these name studies as a book was personal. I wanted this book in my library for future edification, encouragement and enjoyment. I trust that as you read this book, GOD will speak to you as he has me and you too will find the precious nuggets of truth in *What's in a name?* as helpful as I am.

Dr. Bruce Kaufmann, Clearwater Florida

Dedication

To my sons and daughters in the faith:

For the past 50 years I have been blessed to be in ministry, and have been especially privileged to see many come into a personal relationship with God. My calling has been to "make disciples" and God has directed me to invest my life in those who "come behind."

My assignment is not finished until I see those disciples fulfilling their calling and making disciples of those God brings within their influence.

Those I have been helpful to nurture into ministry now span the globe, laboring not only in many venues in America but in dozens for world areas. Those blessings extend into many countries in Africa where I have shared duties in teaching in Bible Schools and directing pastors' conferences.

My prayer is for those generations of sons and daughters to be multiplied.

What's In a Name: Aaron
Exodus 4:14

When God was in the process of commissioning Moses to go lead the Exodus, Moses reminded God of his weaknesses and shortcomings. As it is quite common even with people today, he felt like he was a poor public speaker. Talking to sheep and sagebrush for 40 years does little to refine one's oratorical skills. When Moses realized he would need to confront the Pharaoh, he protested to God, "Please, Lord, I have never been eloquent (a man of words) neither recently, nor in time past, nor since Thou hast spoken to thy servant; for I am slow of speech and slow of tongue." (Ex 4:10) Even though God had the ability to fix Moses problem, he acceded to Moses' plea and recruited his brother, Aaron, to be his spokesman.

In contrast to the very specific meanings of most of the names of the Hebrew children, the name Aaron has no known derivation. Perhaps like many of the names of today, they are chosen for how they sound. While it may not have been intentional by his parents, his name somehow defined his life. We would describe him as endowed with the "gift of gab;" he seemed to always have something to say even if the content was thin.

While Aaron was granted a prominent position, high priest, it appears the selection was based on nepotism and not depth of character. (Some practices in the church are hard to discontinue.) Aaron was quite capable of doing any of the assignments given to him. But he rarely received any communication from God and initiating positive action was not in his repertoire. Rather, he was of a disposition that was easily swayed by others' opinions and when he should have been strong spiritually, he wilted. The demonstration of the fickleness of the Israelites is compelling. In this case where Moses was on the mountain receiving the Ten Commandments on stone, the people couldn't hold steady for even 40 days. They went to Aaron and said, "Make us a God." (Ex 32:1) Aaron didn't even try to argue them out of their hasty and foolish request. He enabled it and made the Golden calf. Aaron "fashioned it with engraving tool;" "he built an altar;" and "he made a proclamation." (32:4–5)

Later Aaron was sucked in by his sister's critical attitude and joined her in defaming Moses. Aaron showed no spiritual backbone, and even loyalty to his brother seemed to escape him. (See Num 12) His plea, "do not account this sin, in which we acted foolishly," (12:11) shows he didn't wish to be responsible or suffer consequences of his actions. It was similar to his lame excuse with the golden calf when Moses confronted him, "what did this people do to you?" (32:21) Aaron's excuse? "You know the people yourself that they are prone to evil." (v 22)

Opportunities to be strong for God were all wasted. Aaron, with the opportunity to define the name by godly character, continued to wander aimlessly through life. His death is covered by just part of verse, "there Aaron died and there he was buried." (Dt 10:6) "There" refers to Moserah, an area in the wilderness, symbolic of the philosophical wilderness in which he lived. His "rod that budded" is mentioned in the New Testament (He 9:4) but Aaron received no billing at all. It takes more than an elegant tongue to leave a legacy. Those who desire more than show are put into the rigors of character development and God grades our tests. Make your name mean something by God's grace!

What's In a Name: Abraham
Genesis 17:5

When Abram responded to God's call, he became the father of the Jewish nation. As the tenth generation from Noah, his family was well settled in Ur of the Chaldees. God never reveals the basis on which Abram was chosen to begin the special group. Abram's father, Terah, had believed his son was special and gave him the name Abram, which means "exalted father." No doubt Terah had hoped Abram would have some great sons who would bring honor and fame to him. But Terah died without seeing grandchildren through Abram.

Abram was 75 years old when he was called by God and the call seemed to enforce the name given by his father. "I will make you a great nation...make your name great." (Gen 12:2) He was to become a father of a nation. But that initial promise did not include the promise to have a direct heir, or a son. It was about ten years of walking with God before he received the expectation that "one who shall come forth from your own body, he shall be your heir." (15:4) A careful reading of the scripture does not indicate Abram even asking for a son. In his own thinking he was too old so he probably didn't even consider the possibility.

God's will was revealed to him that not only was he to have a son, but descendants would become as numerous as the stars of the heavens. (15:5) Even though Abram and Sarai got a little anxious and tried to help God out with the Ishmael birth 14 years before the son of promise was born, they stayed with God's program. At 99 years of age God talked to Abram again and promised that "I will multiply you exceedingly." (17:2)

Abraham had already proven himself as a faithful follower of God, but God wasn't concerned about Abram being honored; his role was to be a father in a biological sense and also in the spiritual realm, not just the founder of a nation. So God felt a name change was in order and dubbed him Abraham, meaning father of multitudes. In the physical sense there have been millions of Jews who have descended from Abraham.

That concept was certainly expanded in the New Testament as he was also considered the "father of faith." "To those who are of the faith of Abraham, the father of us all." (Rom 4:16) It is the power of that faith that reproduces in us the life which "calls into being that which does not exist." (4:17) Abraham's life is so impactful that he is referred to in eleven books in the New Testament, including all four of the gospels.

People of this world, including those in the church, often clamor for position or recognition. But those things are relatively unimportant in the Kingdom of God. Paul contrasted those who wanted to be tutors, but the greatest role in the kingdom is a father who can reproduce his faith in another. "For if you were to have countless tutors in Christ, yet you would not have many fathers for in Christ Jesus I became your father through the gospel." (1 Cor 4:15)

We have way too many who are content to be Abrams (exalted father) but we desperately need Abrahams. The generations who have been lost because they have no father of faith is staggering. The God of Abraham became the God of Isaac who became the God of Jacob. How many generations of faith can you father?

What's In a Name: Absalom
2 Samuel 3:3

When David first became king he was headquartered in Hebron and he fathered six sons while there. The third son was named Absalom. David and his wife Maacah (whose name means depression) began to focus on the future. In contrast to David's war-torn history, the king really desired peace. The name Absalom is a variation of two Hebrew words, abba and shalom, meaning "father of peace." As David reflected on who might succeed him, he had high hopes that it would usher in a time of peace.

That did eventually happen through son number 10, Solomon (peaceful). If you subscribe to the birth order characteristics, the third child usually displays a competitive spirit vying for both recognition and superiority. Absalom fits the bill quite well. When Absalom's sister, Tamar, is sexually violated he takes a revengeful attitude and murders the offender, his brother Amnon. Thus began his "career" of no peace. As a result of his crime, he was a fugitive for the next three years. (2 Sam 13:38) When he finally returned to Jerusalem, he not only had not come to terms with either himself or his father, he created a conspiracy to overthrow his father and proclaim himself as king. His conspiracy began as a political campaign to steal the heart of his countrymen. (2 Sam 15:6) Having built his political base, he launched a frontal attack and King David was caught by surprise and forced to flee.

From every biblical record, Absalom was a troubled young man. When a person cannot come to peace within himself, he will disturb the peace of all within his sphere of influence. Soul unrest breeds agitation in relationships and erupts into open conflict. Following his father's departure from the city of Jerusalem, Absalom entered the city with a lot of pomp. He added insult to injury when he openly "went into" his father's concubines, deliberately provoking the sensibilities of the nation (one of the original "shock-jocks"). (2 Sam 16:21) It seemed at every juncture where a path of peace could be pursued, Absalom chose to go the route of provocation.

Absalom continued to press his case. It was not enough for him to be the king, he wanted to destroy his father. I've seen this same spirit so often in the church, even among leaders who view others as a threat or at least adversarial. They allow their own disturbed spirit to attack others with evil intent to destroy. By continuing the war Absalom placed himself at risk. Ironically, his greatest risk factor was not the military might of his opponents but his own personal pride. One of his badges of pride was his handsome looks, and he focused on his hair. His yearly haircut produced 200 shekels of trimmings (about 5 pounds). (2 Sam 14:26) His hair got caught in the limbs of a tree, and left him hanging, making him an easy target for Joab to slay. (18:9, 14)

David responded with a prolonged time of grief. As a father, I have never lost a child to death, and certainly not under violent circumstances. David's grief was extraordinary because he not only lost a son whom he loved in spite of his waywardness; it was the destruction of a dream. The one he had hoped would be "father of peace" became the epitome of rebellion. Absalom redefined the name by his lifetime of bad choices.

God still looks for those who can father peace.

What's In a Name: Achan
Joshua 7:25

When you meet someone for the first time when they are already an adult, it's challenging to imagine what they were like as a child. I've known some children who seem to either precipitate a disaster or discover one and plop down in the middle of it. When a child who has such a reputation appears I have heard others exclaim, "Uh oh, here comes trouble."

I don't know if Achan was one of those children, but something happened that caused his mother to name him, Achan, which means "trouble." Whether his birth was a troubled event, or whether his mother anticipated the future, we are not told. We are also left to speculate concerning the intervening years prior to his committing a sin of national impact.

Achan was apparently a soldier whose service was neither noted for incompetence or excellence. He simply fulfilled the expectations General Joshua had for him. Prior to the battle of Jericho, instructions were given. "The city shall be under the ban, it and all that is in it belongs to the Lord.... Keep yourselves from the things under the ban, lest you covet them and take some..." (Josh 6:17–18)

Joshua understood that coveting was an issue of the heart and could not be seen by human eyes. He knew that "taking some" was the result of the sin, and such failure would "make the camp of Israel accursed and bring trouble on it." (v 18)

The biblical record states the "sons of Israel acted unfaithfully" (Josh. 7:1) which means covertly or with treachery. The sin of coveting is covert and involves attitudes which though unseen are powerfully destructive. Even though a person may conform to rules or restrictions, their future can be predicted by what they "delight in." If a person's desires are not given over to God, and then replaced by heavenly desires, we are destined to be victimized by our sinful desires. If you don't want what God wants for your life, trouble is your destination.

If you become an Achan (troubler), you can never do it in isolation. There is a philosophical debate in our country about "victimless crimes," but there has never been a victimless sin. Its impact goes far beyond its destruction of the sinner and affects every relationship we have whether they are aware of our sin or not. For Achan, the consequence of this sin was quick and harsh. To his credit, he made a full confession.

Some stories in the Bible are given for our encouragement and some, like Achan, are given as a warning. Achan saw a "beautiful mantle," "coveted it," yielded to the temptation and took it and then concealed it in the ground beneath his tent. (7:21)

Yielding to sin always results in trouble. Even though we may have been named something, it does not need to be a self-fulfilling prophecy. Heredity and environment do not dictate our destiny. Personal choice does and God gives us that power to choose. The place where Achan was executed was then named the "Valley of Trouble.". (7:26)

If you let God conquer your heart and its affections, you can avoid the "Valley of Trouble." By grace you can live above your name!

What's In a Name: Ahab
1 Kings 16:28

Babies are always born with a hope. In the case of King Omri, he would have had several sons to give him hope. For one thing, he was looking for a successor to the throne. But it seems he was more focused on getting a "pal." By naming his son Ahab, which means "friend of his father," his motive becomes clear.

Omri was just another wicked king in the line of monarchs of the Northern Kingdom, Israel. Each king seemed to find new ways to offend God. "Omri did evil in the sight of the Lord, and acted more wickedly than all who were before him." (1 Kings 16:25) He certainly set the pattern well because Ahab took the same cue. "And Ahab the son of Omri did evil in the sight of the Lord more than all who were before him." (v 30) Like father, like son. It is amazing how much of one's life is repeated in his children. Sometimes the things we would like to have done are lived vicariously through our children.

The principle is clear that whatever qualities, good or bad, that we pour over into our children will increase in intensity at least one more step. Many times things are taken to the extreme. Dads want sons to be pals, but kids are looking for heroes. Dads want acceptance from their sons, but sons are hoping for approval from their dads. While the scripture plainly teaches individual responsibility, we are still strongly influenced by our parents.

Our initial view of God is usually associated with our father. Because the home Ahab grew up in had issues, sociologists would say "he didn't have a chance,' that his destiny was set by the early years of formation. In his cases, evil was rampant.

But God doesn't leave evil unrestrained and He intervened in Ahab's life. Ahab had already married Jezebel and erected altars to the false gods of Baal and Asherah. Suddenly he was confronted by the prophet Elijah who foretold of a drought that would last until Elijah said differently. Since "the apple didn't fall too far from the tree," Ahab adopted his father's attitude of ignoring what God said.

Ahab's next encounter with Elijah is a challenge to pit the false prophets against the lone voice for God. Ahab takes the bait and summons the 450 prophets of Baal and 400 prophets of Asherah. Word spread and a huge audience assembled. Elijah accommodated the false prophets with their choice of provisions and time. After an all-day effort by the false prophets, Elijah took just a few minutes to set the stage for "the God who answers by fire" to become their object of worship. Jehovah God came through right on time. This left Ahab without any excuse not to worship the one true God.

Ahab continued to live out his name as a friend of his father. There is no remedy for continued bad choices. Ahab complicated his life by telling "Jezebel all that Elijah had done." (1 Kings 19:1) Any leaning toward repentance was quietly erased by his evil wife. Bad choices seem to multiply, and good patterns of life were only interrupted by his sin. (1 Kings 22:37) The consequences continued to Ahab's 70 sons who all suffered violent deaths. (2 Kings 10:1, 7)

As desirable as it might be, being a friend of your father is inadequate if you're not a friend of the Father.

What's In a Name: Ammiel
Numbers 13:12

Although not a well-known name from the Bible, Ammiel was the name of several men in the Old Testament. One of those was from the tribe of Dan, and was selected by Moses to be one of the twelve spies sent to search out the land of Canaan. It was a great honor to be chosen and then commissioned to make this historic trip and report back to the Israelites in preparation for possessing the land promised to Abraham and his descendants.

The name Ammiel comes from two Hebrew words—the first signifying a tribe or a people group, and the second is one of the words for God (El). So the best translation would be "the people of God." That name would certainly fit in with the concept of a theocracy. Being ruled directly by God, someone who was identified as one of the people of God would be a natural for that kingdom. We already know the Israelites were not a large group of people, but were specially chosen to be God's special nation.

We are familiar with the spies' official report. Of the twelve spies, only two presented the challenge to "go possess the land." Those two were Joshua and Caleb. Ammiel fell prey to the fear that possessed the other ten spies who "discouraged the hearts" of their brothers. "They discouraged the heart of the children of Israel, that they should not go into the land which the Lord had given them." (Num 32:9 KJV)

It is one thing to resist the will of God personally, but it becomes a grievous sin to influence others to follow suit. Others are always watching what we say and do, and tend to mimic what we do.

To be the "people of God" should be an uplifting and fortifying thought. To be loved by the Sovereign of the Universe and considered His possession would be an honor! How does one go from a person designated to inspire others to being a discourager? Discouragement is a very difficult emotion to overcome. It often leads to depression, and the prison bars of that mental state are more confining than maximum security prisons.

There are other Ammiels in the Bible (2 Sam 9:4, 1 Chr 3:5, and 1 Chr 26:5) but none of them had a distinguishing life. Had any of them lived up to their name, history might be different. Think of those people in your life who have been encouraging along your journey. Perhaps because they aren't that many, we tend to remember Encouragers. That is especially true when we encounter deep trials or complicated circumstances or difficult people, and an encouraging word lightens our spirit and renews our hope.

Whatever name you might have been given, you always have a choice to accept the grace of God. Reject God's grace and your destiny is one of defeat. The important thing in this world is not to make a name for ourselves, but to honor God with the best of our ability. Honor yourself, and God will send humbling events into your life. Honor God, and He will find ways to see that you are honored! Even though your name is not Ammiel, you should desire to be of the "people of God."

With God as our King and enabler through abundant grace, we can bless a world and achieve great things for God!

What's In a Name: Amos
Amos 1:1

The prophet Amos did his work for a brief time around 750 BC. God at times used persons during most of their life, but Amos seemed to have a specific message for a specific time and he faithfully delivered it for a few days. Not coming from a noted family or one with any priestly connection proved to be a benefit for Amos.

The circumstances of that age mirrored many other times in history and it certainly includes our present generation. There were social extremes of comfortable prosperity contrasted with abject poverty. As happens so often, the poor were exploited by greedy and dishonest merchants. The judicial system was corrupt throughout the country. Religious leaders had an air of arrogance. Those who had a degree of wealth had been lulled into great apathy. As they did in that era, religious leaders of institutional churches today make it clear they do not want anyone from the fringes calling them to account for their lackadaisical attitudes toward sin.

Amos was a shepherd and a farmer. God is not limited to using people with professional credentials. God was looking for an individual who would respond with simple obedience and availability. The assignment, although it was simple to understand, was not easy. Many times people are willing to do what God wants if it seems to fit or if there is going to be some special blessing. An old adage reminds us that "God does call the qualified; He qualifies the called."

The name Amos means "burdensome." It's difficult to convey the same meaning as was understood by the Hebrews. It suggests a responsibility that is difficult to accomplish. We see it as an odious obligation or duty. Our current culture is famous for shifting responsibilities, often called "passing the buck." But Amos appears to respond favorably and immediately to the vision which God gave him. He knew it would be tough to challenge the wealthy of that day, and declare the judgments of God. But having accepted the assignment, he let nothing deter him from fulfilling God's word.

When the priest of Bethel, Amaziah, asked him to leave and go some other place to deliver his prophecy, he refused. (Amos 7:10-16) He remained faithful to communicating the vision of judgment, no matter how he personally felt or others responded. We often let fear rule us and fail to get the job done, paralyzed with that fear. It would seem to me that Amos had no personal ax to grind with anyone so he was not intimidated by those who opposed his message.

Even when God gives us a job that we don't necessarily love, we must pursue it even it means declaring the judgments of God on the sinfulness of those in our society. But God still has as His ultimate mission to redeem humanity, not punish them. Thus Amos was permitted to end his prophecy with predicting the restoration of Israel. Genuine revival must have genuine repentance as its antecedent. God never overlooks or ignores the sin in our personal lives or the evil in society.

Amos, in living up to his name, carried out his burdensome responsibility of the message of judgment, but ended with the great themes of God's heart: mercy, love, and restoration! (See Amos 9:11-15)

What's In a Name: Ananias
Acts 9:10, 22:12

You've often heard the term "seeking the favor of" which is generally directed toward someone who is rich, powerful, or connected. So much of what happens in our society has little to do with one's ability, wisdom, or initiative. We live in a world of "who do you know." The name Ananias means "favored by God" and comes from a root word meaning to renew.

It would seem by today's psychological standards that being known as "favored by God" that this would be a boon to one's self-image. In a sense we have all received favor from God just in terms of mercy and grace. But Ananias' parents wanted to emphasize that their son was especially favored by God.

Although there were several men with this name, the one we focus on today was a devout disciple living in Damascus. He had a good reputation from the Christian community and was available to God for various assignments. He listened to God as He spoke in a vision one night and told him to go see Saul. Although he had terrible misgivings based on the reputation of Saul, he nevertheless accepted this difficult assignment. Ironically, Ananias did not know until he arrived on Straight Street that his life was not at risk.

When we receive an assignment from God, it will generally be viewed as beyond our capability. If your assignment does not require faith, you can be sure it is not God's project. These special assignments also require that we overcome fear to proceed. Courage is not the absence of fear, but the resolve and power to overcome it. By being obedient, Ananias was part of an unfolding miracle, where the greatest enemy of God was transformed into a power advocate for the kingdom.

Ananias probably did not rate himself high on his performance that day with Saul. He prayed, pronounced a blessing, saw Saul's blinded eyes receive sight, and saw him baptized. In effect, he commissioned him for the work Saul (Paul) was to do in the future. Sometimes God allows us to have a small but important contribution to someone's life whom we discover later is "God's chosen vessel."

Favor (one of the definitions of grace) is God energizing us with a grace endowment. It certainly renews our spirit, often our mind and body also. All by itself, it is renewing. One of those divine principles we so often miss is that grace expands as it is given away. In this case Ananias was the giver, but probably benefitted as much as Saul did. The more we bless and commission others in the kingdom, the more our own faith and character grow.

We have the option to continually "seek" the favor of God. And God answers those requests—we are encouraged more than once to "ask."

How many opportunities are missed because people aren't listening to God? . Many more are missed because we are too fearful to obey God. Still others are looking for others to bless them, not realizing we are the most blessed when we are blessing others. Maybe we need to have the scales removed from our eyes so we can see what and in whom God is working.

Get with God's program!

What's In a Name: Andrew
Matthew 4:18

As Jesus begins his public ministry, he invites twelve men to be his disciples. One of the first ones to respond to the invitation was Andrew. Andrew had been a disciple of John the Baptist, but when John pointed him to the "Lamb of God" Andrew immediately responded and began following Jesus. So Andrew and John (the gospel writer) were the first two to become Jesus' disciples. (See John 1:35-40)

Once having made that decision, Andrew responded by going and finding his brother, Simon Peter. "He first found his own brother Simon, and said to him, "We have found the Messiah" (which is translated, the Christ). And he brought him to Jesus." (John 1:41-42 NKJV) Given the prominence to which Peter rose in the early church, it is noteworthy that Andrew was the one who led him to Christ.

The name Andrew (from the Greek) means "manly" or a man's man. We generally think of manliness as strength and bravery. With Andrew being a fisherman by trade in the context of that geographical area, it would certainly suggest those two characteristics.

Bethsaida was their home town and it was on the north shore of the Sea of Galilee. Because of its unique positioning with the mountains, winds can quickly cause that sea to become turbulent, and it would take both physical strength and mental toughness to endure in that occupation.

There are several other pictures created by the words of scripture to give us insight into Andrew's character. He was industrious in his work. He showed decisiveness when given the invitation by Jesus. "And they immediately left the nets and followed him." (Mt 4:20) Some time later when Jesus was preaching to the multitude, they were confronted with the problem of nothing to feed the crowd. It was Andrew who found the lad with five loaves and two fish, and told Jesus, believing that Jesus could do something with those small provisions. (Jn 6:8-9)

Always looking for opportunity to serve the kingdom he was the one available when the Greeks were looking for Jesus. Philip brought the request to Andrew, who in turn took it to Jesus. (Jn 12:33) Andrew showed the qualities of humility as well as resourcefulness. With each encounter, he showed the lack of selfishness and the willingness to allow others to have the limelight. He was also quite faithful, and was a strong participant in the upper room on the day of Pentecost. (Acts 1:13)

"Men" are depicted in the scripture as those who do not succumb to fear. In the face of enemy warriors, the Israelites were instructed, "Conduct yourselves like men, and fight!" (1 Sam 4:9 NKJV) Andrew lived up to his name by consistently finding a way to invest in the lives of others. Our culture distinguishes itself with the moral and character failures of politicians, businessmen, and religious leaders.

The greatest measure of a man is not in how strong he appears in the face of trials and challenges in his life. Manliness in the biblical sense is best shown in the strength of his legacy lived out in his offspring, both physical and spiritual!

What's In a Name: Aquila
Acts 18:2

We are introduced to Aquila and his wife Priscilla in the book of Acts when Paul finds them in Corinth. They had moved from Rome when Claudius had ordered all Jews to leave Italy. (Acts 18:1-3) Aquila and Priscilla seem to be leaders in the church from the outset. Paul mentions them in three of his epistles (Romans, 1 Corinthians, and 2 Timothy). How and when they came to Christ is not mentioned but they seem to have adjusted to the emperor's order and never again tried to return to Italy. Apparently all their Jewish relatives departed for friendlier territories.

Both Aquila and Priscilla have Latin derived names, which suggests they were born in Italy or strongly influenced by Roman culture. The name Aquila means "eagle." There has been so much written about eagles that I won't attempt to repeat all of that. Among birds of prey, the eagle is considered the strongest. That is a fitting illustration considering the times in which they lived.

From the time of Stephen's martyrdom in Acts 7, persecution was severe. In difficult times, eagles refuse to succumb. They respond to storms by soaring above them. They are able to reach lofty heights without even flapping their wings. By spreading their wings instead of hunkering down, the adverse winds are used to lift them continuously higher.

The church generally had no place to meet, so leaders like Aquila had church in their home. (See 1 Cor 16:19) A study of the rest of early church history, as well as current challenges such as mainland China, documents that the church thrives when times are most difficult. Aquila is not pictured in scripture as being an orator such as Apollos. He certainly did not have the authority or scope of his mentor, Paul. Nevertheless he and his wife were mightily used of God in the early church because of their dedication to Jesus. Faithfulness in the ordinary is often used by God to become the extraordinary!

One of the critical qualities needed for Christians in difficult times is the ability to stand alone. All of us appreciate support when we are going through difficult times. But we are called to demonstrate that God's grace is sufficient to see us through every circumstance, even if others do not join us. When we find that Jesus is all we have left, we find that He is enough!

How many people have yielded to peer pressures, whether inside the church, or in secular society (political correctness)? The character of the eagle is to be unconcerned what other birds choose. When one's heart is fixed on Jesus and His righteousness, the winds of life will not blow us off course however strong.

Early church evangelization beginning with Jesus did not attempt to portray Christianity as easy and prosperous. It is a call to suffering, to self-denial, and to hard work. It's not the kind of enticement towards which flock birds will gravitate. It is an eagle which responds to that type of challenge. Aquila seems to have lived up to his name. His example is a clarion call to today's church for eagles to lead the church in today's hostile environment. Many times they must resist those within the church who desire to take it easy.

Here is the pertinent question for you today: What kind of bird are you in the Kingdom?

What's In a Name: Balaam
Numbers 22:5

When God is working, word gets around. The Israelites has advanced to the plains of Moab. Their game plan did NOT include battling the Moabites; nevertheless, the king, Balak, and his people were "in great fear" and dread because of their mere presence. Balak, whose name means waster, knew he did not have the military strength to fight Israel so he looked for other options. He had heard of a man named Balaam from the town of Pethor in Mesopotamia on the Euphrates River. Balaam, whose name means "not of the people, or foreigner," had a reputation. Balaam was known as the man whose blessings or curses on someone came true. So Balak wanted to hire Balaam to put a curse on Israel. (Num 22:6)

The story has a lot of drama beginning with the delegation sent by Balak to "hire" Balaam. The world operates on a philosophy that anyone can be bought if you make the price high enough. When the king's offer was first presented Balaam did not jump to accept it. Even though Balaam was a foreigner, he seemed to be acquainted with Jehovah God. He was like so many people today who want God when there's a tangible benefit, but they want to have options when they don't like what God has to say.

After Balaam's refusal came, Balak upped the ante with more money and with fame. The second time around Balak sent his distinguished leaders and Balaam caved in. He justified his going by promising only to do what wasn't contrary to the command of God. (Num 22:18) His travel to the land of Moab is a legendary trip. God enabled his donkey first to see the avenging angel, and then to speak intelligently to Balaam.

When he finally had his eyes opened to the warnings that God was graphically giving, he nevertheless continues believing he's obtained God's blessing, not just permission. True to his word, Balaam blesses Israel, not just once, but four times, much to Balak's dismay.

When Satan cannot get at us with a frontal attack, he schemes his way through a side door. Balaam apparently advised Balak that it would take a little time, but Israel could be tempted morally. "While Israel remained at Shittim, the people began to play the harlot with the daughters of Moab. (Num 25:1) What we deny ourselves, we often accommodate in our offspring.

Sin is always multi-dimensional. In this case, fornication was the avenue to idolatry. "They invited the people to the sacrifices of their gods, and the people ate and bowed down to their gods." (v 2) When there are moral deficiencies in character, people worship the idols of money, fame, leisure, etc. As with many medical issues, we only want to treat the symptoms, when God has a complete cure.

Balaam's name initially only meant foreigner, but he defined it by his life. It became the symbol of a "false teacher, who loved the wages of unrighteousness." (2 Pet 2:15) Jude refers to the "error of Balaam" meaning that after you've won the battle, you can lose the war to moral decay. (Jude 11) Even Revelation has a clear warning against the "teaching of Balaam" that put a stumbling block of immorality in the church. (Rev 2:14) While Balaam is remembered, it's never in a good light.

"Foreigner" wasn't such a bad moniker to begin life, but Balaam is forever spoken in disdain because of the corrupting teachings of the man.

What's In a Name: Barnabas
Acts 4:35

The early church in Jerusalem was driven by love to helping each other. Those who owned extra land were motivated to sell it and donate the proceeds to the church so that needs could be met. One of the men who gave was Joseph, a Levite from Cyprus. Though Joseph was his given name, somewhere along his journey others had dubbed him Barnabas, because of his character. Barnabas had a reputation for his upbeat communication and his personal intervention when others needed a help hand. Even though he was written about many times in Acts and other epistles, he is never referred to as Joseph again.

Following this initial notation of who he is, Barnabas re-emerges after the conversion of Saul (Paul). Paul was so effective in proclaiming the gospel, that "the Jews plotted together to do away with him" (Acts 9:23) and his disciples helped him escape through an opening in the city wall of Damascus. (v 25) His coming to Jerusalem was frightening to the disciples there; "they were all afraid of him, not believing that he was a disciple." (v 26) It was here that Barnabas accepted the risk and "took hold of him and brought him to the apostles" (v 27) and told Paul's story with conviction.

Barnabas' reputation was sufficient to get Paul accepted in Jerusalem. The persecution that followed Stephen's death caused the disciples to leave Jerusalem and many went to Antioch. As a result, they sent Barnabas there to check on the "revival" that had occurred. He recognized the authenticity of God's moving, and "rejoiced and began to encourage (exhort) them." (11:23) These examples show why he had earned the name Barnabas, which means "son of Encouragement" (4:36) or Consolation. While some need more encouragement than others, I've never met anyone who did not benefit from encouragement. To encourage means to inspire or stimulate courage, spirit or hope.

Even while Barnabas was giving new strength to the church at Antioch he did not see Paul. Paul had gone back to his home in Tarsus. So Barnabas went to Tarsus and brought Paul back with him and mentored him there for an entire year in teaching at the gatherings. While Paul may have been the more highly educated one, he had a lot to learn from Barnabas' people skills and his gift of encouragement. Barnabas kept Paul with him when they visited Jerusalem to deliver the financial gifts to help the impoverished in Judea. (11:30) Having fulfilled their mission in Jerusalem (12:25), they returned to Antioch.

Since Antioch had become the center of Christian activity, it was only natural they would be the first sending church of a missionary team. Guided by the Holy Spirit, the church "set apart" Barnabas and Paul as a team. So this duo blazed the trail in that first missionary journey. A disagreement over Barnabas' nephew, John Mark, prevented the team from subsequent trips. (15:39) Both men simply chose new partners and the missionary efforts doubled. Barnabas took Mark, even with his previous desertion, and encouraged and molded him into a stalwart leader who subsequently became a gospel writer. Mark is also mentioned in the letter by Paul to Timothy as "useful to me for service." (2 Tim 4:11)

This Son of Encouragement played a critical role in the early church, particularly in redeeming those that others rejected!

What's In a Name: Bezaleel
Exodus 31:2

Sometimes we don't think of God as the source of all knowledge, even when we affirm the doctrine of omniscience. But God has infinite awareness, understanding, and insight. He is possessed with universal or complete knowledge. When we think there is a "new" idea, thing, or process we must acknowledge that it has been "discovered." The truth lay beneath the surface and we finally dug deep enough to make our great discovery.

I have often thought about "who taught the teachers?" Who began any of the disciplines, whether math, science, medicine, engineering, and craftsmanship? When Israel was extricated from Egyptian bondage, God wanted many things built that had not previously been done. So just as God had called Moses to his work, "the Lord spoke to Moses, saying, 'See, I have called by name, Bezaleel, the son of Uri, the son of Hur, of the tribe of Judah." (Ex 31:2) Bezaleel means "in the shadow of God," which the Hebrews understood as "under the protection of God."

Even though in the philosophy of many, there is a demarcation between sacred and secular, God views His world as "good" or righteous. Christians are to do all for the glory of God. (1 Cor 10:31) When we examine what God was placing in Bezaleel, we stand in awe. Creativity is one of the marks of the divine.

And God said, "I have filled him with the Spirit of God in wisdom, in understanding, in knowledge, and in all kinds of craftsmanship." (31:4) God gets the order of acquisition right. Wisdom, a gift from God for the asking, (Jam 1:5) needs to precede understanding. In the framework of wisdom and understanding, knowledge becomes useful and then skills or craftsmanship can be developed. (See this same order in Prov 24:3-4.) Only in the context of this order does creativity glorify God and benefit mankind.

Bezaleel's ability was not confined to just one medium. God gave him the skills "to make artistic designs for work in gold, in silver and in the carving of wood, that he may work in all kinds of craftsmanship." (Ex 31:4-5) Anyone who has actually worked in various metals knows that skills must be divergent. And there is a great difference between working with the varieties of wood.

God was not asking Moses for his opinion in this matter, and He even exercised authority to designate him to this position. "I, Myself, have appointed" (v 6) even the helper. When the craftsmanship of ancient civilizations is discovered, we marvel at how they were able to achieve what they did. Our generation goes directly to acquiring knowledge, but we all know knowledge does not engender creativity. More information does not inspire.

We all know smart people who display no common sense, often making bad decisions. God protects or shadows the special gifts that He places in people. And when men such as Bezaleel are content to work under that protection, they can produce awe-inspiring work that transcends the ages. Knowing God's commission, Moses "called Bezaleel and Oholiab and every skillful person in whom the Lord had put skill, everyone whose heart stirred him, to come to the work to perform it." (Ex 36:2)

Don't waste your God-given talents!

What's In a Name: Caleb.
Numbers 13:6, 30

We are first introduced to Caleb when he was selected to be one of the 12 spies to go evaluate the land of Canaan. Representing the tribe of Judah, one of the largest of the tribes, Caleb distinguished himself as a man of character. The qualification for being chosen as a spy was prior leadership in their respective tribe. (Num 13:6). Parents of that day usually chose names for their children based on heritage or character. If character was the choice, it was usually into what the parents hoped the child would do develop.

Experience has shown that sometimes a name may define a person, but more often a person defines the name. The name Caleb basically means "forcible" and in modern parlance would be the word "fortitude." Webster defines fortitude as "strength of mind that enables a person to encounter danger or bear pain and adversity with courage."

All 12 spies started out on equal footing. Chosen by the same criteria, they were all given the same instruction. They were together when they walked and saw the abundance of Canaan. It was God's intention that these spies would be inspired by the great things He had in store for them. Having seen the mighty hand of God in the Exodus, conquering Canaan should have been considered a "no-brainer." Arriving back in the camp, the spies put on a "show and tell." The stories were awesome and were bolstered by the sight of the "single cluster of grapes" from the Valley of Eschol. (Num 25:27)

When the reporting was done, there was a vast divergence in the response of the spies to their own report. Caleb and

Joshua stood apart from the other ten. Old Mr. Fortitude was the spokesman for the "good guys." "We should by all means go up and take possession of it for we shall surely overcome it." (Num 13:30) The name Caleb is also associated with another Hebrew word that means to "yelp like an attack dog." As a stalwart 40-year-old, Caleb was rough and ready. As the son of Jephunnah, it meant "he will be prepared." That implies that Jephunnah was deeply responsible for the readiness in Caleb's mind, body, and spirit to lead the way into Canaan.

The story of the Israelites listening to the ten bad spies and losing heart is legendary. It cost them 40 years of wandering aimlessly in the wilderness, and a certain death sentence. But the real story is that it subjected Caleb to that same 40 years of waiting for God's promise for an inheritance. Caleb had shown the metal in his spine in his spy job, but the real test would come when he would be subjected to the whining and grumbling of over 1 million people for those 40 years. It boggles my mind!

It's difficult to deal with our own missteps and their consequences. And Caleb not only survived this long ordeal, he kept a good attitude. The force within him was more than sufficient to keep his physical strength as well as his fighting spirit. His resiliency is seen in his words, "I am 85 years old. I am as strong this day as I was when Moses sent me; as my strength was then, even so is my strength now, for war, both to go out and to come in. Therefore, give me my mountain..." (Josh. 14:11 – 12).

Anyone who can survive like Caleb has earned his name. I pray that more of that DNA gets passed down to many generations to come.

What's In a Name: Daniel
Daniel 1:6-7

Daniel as a teenager went to Babylon during the first deportation in 606 BC He and several of his close friends were recognized as "youths in whom was no defect, who were good looking, showing intelligence in every branch of wisdom, endowed with understanding, and discerning knowledge, and who had ability for serving..." (Dan 1:4) There are not many young people, then or now, who would be described in such glowing terms.

The name Daniel means "the judge of God" or "one who renders justice by the strength of the Almighty." We don't know about Daniel's birth and adolescent years. But his parents appear to have set the environment for him to have a dynamic relationship to God. While the Babylonian king may not have had criteria of moral goodness for selection to personal service, he recognized the character qualities that served as the foundation for excellence.

The first major encounter for Daniel concerned his diet. King Nebuchadnezzar had "choice food" and wine, which he thought contributed to his elite status. To live up to his name, Daniel needed to incorporate into his life the principles of holy living. So Daniel made up his mind (purposed, resolved) not to violate his conscience. With a wise appeal, he was able to convince the authorities to honor his convictions. God responded by giving "them knowledge and intelligence and every branch of literature and wisdom." (1:17)

Daniel's first big opportunity to live up to his name came when Nebuchadnezzar had a disturbing dream. His memory of the dream faded but the agitated emotions continued. The king ordered his wise men to tell him the dream and interpretation as well. Daniel and his friends averted death by engaging in a night of prayer. (2:17 – 18) God came through in a timely manner, and Daniel was promoted to an authoritative position in this heathen nation where he could fulfill his name as a "judge of God."

The king had another dream and Daniel was forced to reveal God's judgment that was to fall on Nebuchadnezzar. The dream became reality and Nebuchadnezzar left the throne and lived like an animal for the next seven years. Daniel, however, maintained his position with the next monarch who was equally wicked. At a banquet, a mysterious hand showed up to write on the wall. Daniel was called upon to interpret and once again had to declare the judgment of God. That judgment also came true, and Daniel subsequently was privileged to serve under a third king, Darius. Serving God faithfully is no escape from trouble. We are always tempted to take the way of safety for ourselves. Daniel's enemies, who were also in government positions, tricked the King and subsequently Daniel had a chargeable offense for which the penalty was a trip to the lion's den, His crime? Praying! But the God who had declared righteous judgment through Daniel showed he could render judgment for Daniel as well. Even though he had to go into the lion's den, God miraculously shut the mouths of those lions. After a long night, Daniel was taken up out of the den the next morning and no injury was found on him because he had trusted in his God. (Dan 6:23)

Daniel had a great name, and by faith and grace, confirmed that one can live up to his name.

What's In a Name: Deborah
Judges 4:4

Scripture is fascinating in its presentation of certain stories. Beginning in Genesis and carrying through the entire Old Testament, we are shown a male dominant society. However, God inserts little insights along the way that women are indeed quite valuable in terms of faith. One of the remarkable stories in the scriptures is that of the prophetess Deborah who also served as a judge. God is never defensive about using anyone in any situation and He doesn't offer any justifications for His actions. He just tells the story.

Desperate times call for courageous leadership and Deborah, a woman of deep conviction, was available. She was comfortable with simply giving prophetic directions (Jud 4:6, 9) for others to accomplish but Barak wasn't willing to lead the war effort without her personal presence. Working together as a team they were able to see great things accomplished for God and Israel.

One irony is that Barak accepted the Number 2 position, but it is he who is mentioned in the Hall of Faith (Heb 11:32), not Deborah. Great leadership is shown by allowing God to get all the glory. In another of God's ironic twists, neither Deborah nor Barak performed the decisive action that ended the war; it was assigned to another lady, Jael, who slew the enemy captain with a tent peg and a hammer. (Jud 4:21) God can do incredible things when we are not concerned about what person gets the credit.

The name Deborah means "bee," and suggests one being systematic or having orderly motion. Bees are interesting to watch as they fly from flower to flower to extract nectar. They are very focused, do their collecting and then return to the hive. There they are joined with other "worker" bees to convert the nectar to honey. Compare their activity with that of a fly which seeming flits around aimlessly, often returning to the same place. Another comparison is a gnat which also emits an annoying buzz.

We can learn some significant principles from the bees.
- Remember that your purpose is to collect nectar, not smell the roses.
- If the nectar is gone, move on to the next flower.
- It is not motion that achieves, but purposeful action.
- Your timely work should be the distraction, rather than others distracting you.

You should make every flap of the wings move you towards success.. Deborah was a great example of not allowing distractions to lure her off the course that God had designed.

God uses all kinds of leadership, but in this case it was not a charismatic personality that was needed. Deborah had to go with the men into war, and give timely and specific instruction without getting rattled. She may have had natural gifting in this area (which is also a gift of God's grace), but it also required special grace.

Faithfulness, availability, and humble attitudes are the key ingredients to which God looks in us when He needs to send a miracle. Without them, God cannot use us and the Kingdom suffers.

Deborah lived up to her name, and did so in a very God-honoring way!

What's In a Name: Elijah
1 Kings 17:1

Although the first mention of the prophet Elijah is a major confrontation with King Ahab, he must have been active in the nation of Israel for several years prior. As a prophet of God, he seems to deliver the messages he received. Because of the sins of the king and the people, those pronouncements were warnings. To Ahab he was labeled as the "troubler of Israel." (1 Kings 18:10)

While priesthood was limited to the tribe of Levite, prophets were from every part of the nation. God was simply looking for willing vessels who would deliver God's word in spite of their fear, personality quirks, or recognition. Prophets did not go before some "official board" to get a prophet's license. Authenticity was determined by whether or not their message came true every time. In other words, God himself validated His chosen ones.

Elijah has a very interesting name, a blend of two Hebrew words for God. "El" was one of the designations for God meaning "the Almighty" and alludes to His strength and sovereignty. The latter part is "jah" which is the short version of "YHWH," or Jehovah. So his name means "God, Jehovah." Whether this name was given to him as an honor to God, or whether it was expressed as a hope he would live righteously, we don't know. We are given no details of his early life. He simply arrives on the scene as a seasoned spokesman for Jehovah.

One characteristic of most godly persons is they have extensive private time with God, not just the public spotlight. So right after he delivered the "no rain" speech to King Ahab, God tells him to "Go away from here." (1 Kings 17:1-2) Delivering a convicting message can be an energy draining event. In spite of the boldness that Elijah displays, those were times of God-empowerment. James tells us Elijah was an ordinary man "subject to like passions as we are." (James 5:17) His name may have helped him focus at times, but he was still grace dependent. Every time someone called him by name, he heard the name of God twice. That could have been both inspiring and convicting.

Elijah's life is mixed with highs and lows emotionally. He was given small but rewarding assignments such as going to the widow in Zarephath. (1 Kings 17:9) There we have God supplying on an as needed basis. Jesus mentions this event, that there were "many widows in Israel in the days of Elijah" and yet Elijah was sent….only to that one. (Lk 4:25-26)

Elijah had his low times as well. Following a very real threat by Jezebel, Elijah went to hide and faced depression so severe he begged God to take his life. (1 Kings 19:4) That emotional drain was right after he had won the great victory against the 850 prophets of Baal and Asherah.

One of the great successes of Elijah was his invitation to Elisha, who responded enthusiastically. The spirit of Elijah was inborn through the mentoring years until Elijah was taken away. Elisha witnessed the "chariots of fire and horses of fire" which took Elijah to heaven in a windstorm. (2 Kings 2:11)

So this life lived for God was punctuated by an exclamation point! His life illustrated his name and gave glory to the God he served.

What's in the name: Elisha
1 Kings 19:19

As Elijah began to think about leaving this earth, he found a young man out plowing in the field. He must've been experienced because of his skill in directing 12 pairs of oxen. When Elijah threw his mantle on Elisha, Elisha understood the gesture and was fully agreeable to going with the old prophet. But he was also considerate enough to go back and kiss his parents goodbye. (1 Kings 19:20) Perhaps when he was born, his parents expressed the strong belief and hope that God would hear their prayers against the evils of their days so they named him Elisha, meaning "a God who hears supplication" (earnest and humble prayer).

The primary means of learning at that time was to live with a teacher. It was not considered a full education if one could only recite data or information. By being with the mentor 24/7, an instructor could give the application of knowledge to real-life situations. In this classroom of one, the subject matter was inclusive of all the surroundings and Elisha took it all in.

While there were "schools of the prophets" at Bethel, Jericho, and other places, Elisha was considered privileged to be a protégé of Elijah. On the journey to meet the fiery chariot, Elijah and Elisha seem to understand what was to happen as did the sons of the prophets along the way. (2 Kings 2:3)
There is an interesting contrast regarding the mantle. When Elijah first called Elisha he did so by throwing his mantle on him. When Elijah was taken away, his mantle fell down but it did not fall Elisha. It fell on the ground and Elisha had to pick it up. (2 Kings 2:13) We might receive some kind of designation at times but if we're going to possess the mantle we have

personal responsibility. Elisha did not choose to follow Elijah simply to carry on the work. As he personally observed the spirit of his mentor and understood the awesome power of God working in and through him, it made him hungry for God. Elijah opened the opportunity for him when he said to him, "Ask what I shall do for you before I am taken from you." (2:9) Elisha was quick to respond, "Please, let a double portion of your spirit be upon me." I've observed the passing of generations before and the scene is usually quite different. When there has been an extraordinary man of spirit, those coming along have often said, "Oh, if I could just be half the man he's been, I'd be thrilled." And many have accepted that. But when each generation is only half the former in spirit, it doesn't take long for the reservoir to run dry.

Where are the men who can impact the world, a generation, or even a church? Elisha's simple but earnest request was honored. He immediately felt the power of God flow through him as he approached the Jordan River without the physical presence of Elijah for the first time. He struck the waters just as he had seen his mentor do, and God responded by parting the waters. That was the beginning of a life of miracles in military assistance, assisting the widow, raising a son back to life, and healing leprosy. By the time he died, he had almost done twice as many miracles as his predecessor. God is true to his word, but Elisha was one short when he was buried. A short time later during the military skirmish, the Army was forced to throw a body into the same grave as Elisha's bones. "And when the man touched the bones of Elisha, he revived and stood on his feet." (13:21)

Elisha fulfilled his name by continual supplication to his God, not just the God of Elijah.

What's In a Name: Ezekiel
Ezekiel 1:3

Ezekiel, as a young man, was among those carted off to Babylon in the second deportation in 597 BC. He had been there just a little over four years when "the word of the Lord came expressly to Ezekiel, the priest." (Eze 1:3) Already one who was dedicated to God's service, he was given this added responsibility of a prophet which would last for over twenty years, all of it in Babylon.

Obviously, as a captive of a foreign government, Ezekiel had a great challenge to present a view of a powerful God. Never mind that the bondage had come as a result of persistent long-term sinning, many still expected that God could, should and would deliver quickly. Ezekiel was probably the most colorful of the prophets and resorted to many different means for proclaiming the message. He used pantomime, had various antics such as crying out, wailing, and slapping his thighs. One time he literally ate a scroll, and graphically presented God's word so people would really "get it."

In trying to restore a proper understanding of a holy and transcendent God, it was necessary for Ezekiel to have visions which he describes in terms of the radiance and glory of God. (Eze 1:27-28) When he was called, God gave him the challenge: "I am sending you to them who are stubborn and obstinate children." (Eze 2:4) His ministry would be both revealing and convicting so "they will know that a prophet has been among them." (v 5)

God warned him that the people probably would not listen to him since they wouldn't listen to God anyway. (3:7) Like the other prophets Ezekiel's warnings of doom were not the final disposition of God's people. There was always a hope of restoration when there would be genuine repentance. Ezekiel saw beyond what was to what could be when the transformation would come. Even though the Messiah is not mentioned by designation, the taking of the "heart of stone out of their flesh" and giving them "a heart of flesh" was a clear reference to the effect of the atonement and the power of resurrection. (Eze 11:19; 36:26)

One of the revelations to Ezekiel stressed individual responsibility for one's own sins to an extent unparalleled in Old Testament writings. In contrast to the prevailing thought in Israel that all sins affected the family and the nation, Ezekiel states emphatically "when the son has practiced justice and righteousness and has observed all MY statutes and done them, he shall surely live." (18:19) Ezekiel, by definition, means "God will strengthen." He understood that individuals could choose to be strengthened by God instead of succumbing to society's pressures.

One of the classic stories of Ezekiel is the valley of dry bones. When something has been dead so long the bones are dry, it would take more than simple faith that God could make them alive into a stalwart army. In fulfillment of his name, Ezekiel witnessed that great miracle. Along with that he saw the full restoration of Israel, the Temple, and the land. Material from many of Ezekiel's chapters is either quoted or alluded to in every chapter in Revelation, except one.

In spite of appearances of the trials, tribulations and other energy draining circumstances, we can know that "God will strengthen."

What's In a Name: Ezra
Ezra 7:1

In studying world history, it is fascinating to see events occur that seem extremely unlikely. Time and time again God has shown little regard for CW (conventional wisdom). When Jeremiah's prophecy of seventy years of captivity became reality, there was no one sitting around trying to figure a way to reverse that seventy years down the road. So God arranged a change of empires and worked through a Persian king, Cyrus. The record clearly states that "the Lord (Jehovah) stirred the spirit of Cyrus." (Ezra 1:1) Who would have thought that an ungodly king would be more readily obedient to God's commands than His chosen people?

The focus of those early returnees was to rebuild the temple. After numerous starts and stops over some thirty years, the physical structure had been rebuilt and the temple dedicated. Three Persian kings had successively kept the project authorized. (Ezra 6:14) It was during the reign of Artaxerxes that Ezra left Babylon and journeyed to Jerusalem. While the building was there, the spiritual worship of God had not returned. Ezra "was a scribe skilled in the law of Moses." (7:6) As such he was summoned for special duty.

The name Ezra means "help or aid" and carries the connotation of surrounded by help so as to provide complete protection. Ezra could not have lived up to his name without cooperating with God. While God provides His enabling grace freely, it is most efficacious to those who discipline themselves. "For Ezra had set his heart to study (seek) the law of the Lord, and to practice it, and to teach His statutes and ordinances in Israel." (7:10)

Following this procedure would make a major impact in our churches. Satan has made inroads into the Christian community and our homes in powerful ways. Failure to provide "help" in a timely and effective way has allowed Satan entrance to what should have been sacred.

Ezra first had to "set" his own heart. Setting has to do with both our resolve and our focus and requires us to avoid the distractions of life. Ezra was a determined student of the law and not just to learn it but to implement it in his life. How much different would be our world if the level of obedience was raised to match the level of knowledge!

Satan doesn't care how much scripture is known as long as he can thwart the practice of it. Once having woven the principles of scripture in his life, he was now ready to teach the Israelites. There is nothing like teaching others to clarify and cement principles into our thought processes.

Ezra was concerned about the safety in traveling and fasted and prayed. (Ezra 8:21) His main help to the Israelites was to get them reconciled to God. So much of religion only touches the superficial or surface. Because of Ezra's faithfulness to God by "praying, weeping, and prostrating himself," (10:1) he called on the people to accept responsibility and "be courageous and act." (10:4) Ezra fulfilled his calling, lived up to his name, and brought a nation back to the true worship of God.

We should take courage that God can do something in our generation, even with an unrighteous government, as long as there are ministers like Ezra to "help."

What's in a Name: Gideon
Judges 6:11 – 12

The tribe of Manasseh never achieved much prominence among the other tribes. And in typical pecking order in a family, particularly a Jewish family, the youngest son was afforded no honor. When a spiritual or national crisis occurs, God has never been concerned with what others think. God seems to take pleasure in taking what society rejects and using it for His purposes. And if it isn't a reject, it's usually one whom we would least expect, the ones upon whom they will be looked down.

In the midst of that crisis, God sent an angel to speak directly to Gideon, the baby boy of Joash, and greeted him "the Lord is with you, O valiant warrior." (Jud 6:12) Gideon was not impressed, and promptly asked the angel, "If the Lord is with us, why has all this happened to us?" (v 13) He continued, "and where are all his miracles which our fathers told us about?" The ensuing conversation showed the angel giving Gideon an empowering commission to go defeat Midian. After Gideon gives him a "Are you sure?" question, based on the "least" and the "youngest" arguments (v 15), the angel assures him of God's power. Gideon was willing to accept the assignment, but he wanted the assurance of a sign

God is aware that in national crises, whether political, economic, or health related, that the underlying issue is always spiritual. So Gideon's intermediate assignment was to destroy the altars of Baal and cut down the Asherah which the people had been worshiping. While Gideon was preparing to take on foreign powers he was afraid of his family (v 27) so he carried out the task at night rather than face them in the daylight.

When the city leaders discovered their idols destroyed, they came to Joash and demanded him to turn over his son. Joash showed a lot of wisdom when he responded that if Baal were really a god with power why didn't he defend himself? The city fathers apparently had no answer. (v 31) This event caused Joash to add the name "Jerubabaal" to Gideon, which meant "let Baal contend against him."

Next up was preparing for the battle with Midian and its allies. Accepting a commission from God doesn't automatically come with confidence or courage. Assignments from God will always be beyond our capability. If they weren't, there would be no need for faith. We never find Gideon unwilling or rebellious to do God's will. He merely asked for confirmation so he could proceed confidently. He asked for additional signs such as the double fleece test. (vv 36 – 40)

Gideon meant "warrior" which simply implies someone engaged in battle. God was looking for someone to be valiant, i.e., one with valor and virtue. God's instruction to pare down the volunteers defies CW (conventional wisdom). The fear factor sent 22,000 of the 32,000 home quickly. (7:3) The lapping water test sent another 9700 home leaving Gideon with only 300 men. (7:7) God seems to love impossible odds. As a final confidence builder, God allowed Gideon to go to the enemy's camp and hear the biscuit versus the tent story. (7:13 – 14) God vindicated Gideon emphatically, and retained the glory for Himself.

Gideon wasn't just a warrior, he was God's warrior and that got him named in the hall of faith, "for time would fail me to tell of Gideon." (Hebrews 11:32)

What's In a Name: Habakkuk
Habakkuk 1:1

Some things are so obvious that we hesitate to speak them, but we are all special to God in some unique way. The prophet Habakkuk is rather obscure as a person, but his prophetic utterance is fascinating. He is bold enough to have a stimulating conversation with God in which he questions Him why the wickedness of the Jews hasn't been punished as it should. When God responds that He is about to unleash the Chaldeans on them, Habakkuk reacted, "I didn't mean that much!" (Hab 1:13) He knew of the cruelty of the Chaldeans and asked why God would use such an ungodly nation to accomplish this task.

While God did not answer Habakkuk's question directly He pointed him to compelling truth that His justice and righteousness were intact. "Write the vision…it is yet for an appointed time…..it will not fail…..it will certainly come." (Hab 2:2-3) God does to us what we often do to our children and that is to defer the information while we affirm the relationship.

The name Habakkuk means "embrace, clasp, or enfold." In the vernacular we would call it a hug. So in this process, God simply gave him a hug. Have you ever been hugged by God?

A hug communicates acceptance and value. Often times it represents safety or security. Hugs do wonders for children and are usually more important than words. As Habakkuk was receiving his hug from God, he gained an insight that has reverberated throughout history. It was these simple words, "The just shall live by faith." (2:4)

The Apostle Paul reached back in time and latched on to the nugget of truth and then hurled it 1500 years into the future. (Rom 1:17) Martin Luther in his spiritual struggles against the abuses in the Catholic Church had an epiphany and suddenly "faith" was born into his darkened spirit. He did not express it as such but he had been hugged by God. The church had reduced spirituality to rules and regulations. But the hug sparked the Reformation and birthed a revival of faith.

The hug was so transforming that his perspectives all changed. He had faith to ask that God revive His work. (3:2) He could focus on the radiance of the Almighty, having felt the strength and warmth. Habakkuk's outlook was so radically different that faith blossomed in the night of despair. "Though the fig tree should not blossom, and there be no fruit on the vines, though the yield of the olive should fail, and the fields produce no food, though the flock should be cut off from the fold and there be no cattle in the stalls.." (3:17) were the troubles listed. Your list is probably different but just as desperate. It represents things which are beyond your control.

Impossibilities may appear as deserts to you, but they are the breeding grounds for explosive faith!

The hug from God and the response of faith made him exclaim, "yet I will exult in the Lord, I will rejoice in the God of my salvation." (3:18) Those of us who have stood on the coast and gazed on an ocean of difficulties with no way to cross, feeling the "aloneness" and hopelessness, also know the difference when a loving God sneaks from behind and embraces us with His love.

Be God's emissary and give someone a hug today!

What's In a Name: Haggai
Haggai 1:1

As a contemporary of Zechariah, Haggai prophesied during the same period and their messages were overlapping. Quite often there was only one significant prophet at a time. This era had seen a culture with little motivation. The Babylonian empire had collapsed after holding the Israelites captive for nearly seventy years. There had been a few who responded to the benevolence of the Persian kings and returned to Jerusalem to rebuild the walls with either Nehemiah or Ezra to begin the rebuilding of the temple.

There had been a little start on the temple, but discouragement had stopped any progress for sixteen years. Apparently the people had decided, and were vocal about it, that it just wasn't the right time to work on the temple. They decided to upgrade their personal houses with "paneled" walls, while God's house lay desolate.

Haggai's opening message confronts the Israelites with cogent words. "Consider your ways! You have sown much but harvest little; you eat, but there is not enough to be satisfied; you drink, but there is not enough to become drunk; you put on clothing, but no one is warm enough; and he who earns, earns wages to put into a purse with holes." (Hag 1:5b-6)

While Haggai is addressing their actions, most of his words are directed at the attitudes of the people. When he tells them to quit being lazy and "go up to the mountains, bring wood and rebuild the temple, that I may be pleased with it and be glorified," (1:8) he expresses the real issue of the heart. People will not do something for long if it is not in their heart. In some circumstances where people are compelled to do something, their output is substandard. The same is true in the spiritual realm. When obedience to God is seen as servitude or drudgery, there is no positive development in that person's life. If you want to change someone's behavior temporarily, make a rule. If you want to change someone long-term, change the affections of their heart and behaviors change as a consequence.

The name Haggai means "festive." Festive speaks to a joyful attitude, one that is celebrating life. In today's terms we would call Haggai "the life of the party." Churches quite often resemble mortuaries in their clean but cold environments. When there is no joy in the camp everything becomes twice as hard. Resources seem to dry up. Contrast that with Paul's reminder that "God loves a <u>cheerful</u> (not fearful) giver." (2 Cor 9:7)

When people willingly have a "mind to work" with a whole heart, God is not only pleased, but promises to bless them. (Hag 2:19) Our hands and hearts with God's blessing become a productive combination. Over the succeeding five years, the temple was restored. Haggai and Zechariah are both credited with giving encouragement to the project and seeing it finished.

Zechariah appealed to their conscience and spiritual ideal. Haggai touched their emotions. We need both, but most people are moved to action through their emotions. When you can make those big projects (long and/or hard) into a party, the job gets done quicker and better, with spiritual gusto.

Especially when you've been through wearisome years, it's time to celebrate God's blessing and be festive!

What's In a Name: Hananiah, Mishael, Azariah
Daniel 1:6-7

Sometimes friendships are formed when you're "thrown together" by circumstances not of your own choosing. Of those who were carted off to Babylon, these were three young men who seemed to stick together. Whether they were friends before this event, we are not told. But when you are "yanked" away from your family, friendships become very important. The names of these three men were Hananiah which means "favored of God;" Mishael meaning "essence of God;" and Azariah which declares "God has helped." As soon as they arrived in Babylon, their names were translated into the local language as Shadrach, Meshach and Abednego. Their Babylonian names stuck and are more familiar than their Hebrew ones, but the meanings are the same.

We often see children and youth victimized by unsettling circumstances, and all too often that is used as an excuse to respond with bad attitudes and behaviors. We often refer to these situations as "make or break" ones. Seldom is there an in between outcome. These three men banded together, and though they had some overlapping circumstances with Daniel, their journey had its own unique path.

While God sometimes calls us to stand alone, it is very comforting when God gives us friends. It's even better when our friends go with us through those valleys. The wise man Solomon observed, "if one can overpower him who is alone, two can resist him. A cord of three strands is not quickly torn apart." (Eccl 4:12) The three seemed to do everything together, even speaking in unison! (Dan 3:16) What a trio!

Combining the favor of God with the nature of God and mixing it with the help of God makes a bond so tight that Nebuchadnezzar could not break it. These three seemed to have grasped the ideal of God's plan and committed themselves to it.

Although they had been appointed to leadership roles because of their God-given talents (2:49), that was no exemption from persecution. Instead, it probably made them a target. But even the threat of a fiery furnace was not sufficient to cause them to vacate righteous principles. These men stood firm in their faith that God would deliver them <u>from</u> the blast.

Their combined faith was so strong that they were able to say, "But even if He does not" deliver, they would accept death. Until a person is not afraid to die, he doesn't truly begin to live. God's plan is always different from our presuppositions and in this case deliverance would come <u>in</u> the fire. In this episode of fire, they were treated to a personal audience with God.

Even though we might receive vision and inspiration from a well-chosen name, it is our life's choices that determine our destiny. These men seem to not only have lived up to their names, they added a significantly new dimension. Although they are not mentioned by name in the Hall of Faith, their deed is referred to as by faith they "quenched the power of fire." (Heb 11:34)

The combination of "Favored of God," "nature of God," or "helped by God" may simply be your call to be something great for God!

What's In a Name: Hosea
Hosea 1:1

As with many of the prophets, Hosea was called to deliver a difficult message. The Northern Kingdom, or Israel, had never had a righteous king. The first king of the breakaway tribes was Jereboam who quickly led the nation to worship idols. At the time that Hosea began his ministry another Jereboam was the king and was continuing the evil ways. Hosea was the final prophet before the fall of the Northern Kingdom in 721 B.C. Hosea reminded them of their unfaithfulness, and how they seemed to invent new ways to sin. Yet they were promised restoration when God had finished punishing them.

The name Hosea meant "deliverer" and that was his ultimate message to the Israelites. But God had a special assignment for Hosea that no other prophet before or since has been asked to do. The task was to clearly illustrate God's relationship to Israel. Hosea was instructed to "Go, take to yourself a wife of harlotry, (Hos 1:2) and have children of harlotry." He found Gomer and apparently loved her and temporarily she found satisfaction in the marriage. Hosea fathered a son with her.

Shortly thereafter Gomer slips away and gets pregnant twice from illicit relationships. Even though they were not his, Hosea loved the boy and girl and cared for them as any biological father would do. The names are a clue he knew their true parentage. The girl was named Lo-ruhamah and the boy Lo-ammi. The "Lo" means "not," so the literal translation of Lo-ruhamah is "not obtaining compassion." Lo-ammi means "not my people." (1:6, 9)

As tragic as these details are, they only scratched the surface in depicting Israel's spiritual adultery. Anyone who has experienced the grief of an unfaithful spouse can certainly identify with Hosea. Hosea's love for Gomer is unparalleled in human history. Even with him loving her through her adulteries, she still chose to leave him and seek other lovers. She wasted herself so much that she was eventually treated as a worthless slave and put up for sale. Rejected as even a cheap prostitute, Gomer was repurchased by Hosea for "15 shekels and a homer and a half of barley." (3:2) (Equivalent of about $4 in coins and $25 of barley.)

Hosea wasn't instructed to just buy her as property, but to love her. The full acceptance of Gomer is indicated by Hosea's words, "Then I said to her, 'You shall stay with me for many days. You shall not play the harlot, nor shall you have [another] man; so I will also be toward you.'" (3:3) In our humanity, we struggle to overcome our disappointments of a wayward spouse because trust has been so shattered. Hosea as a "deliverer" rescued Gomer from certain death, just as God did for Israel time and time again. There is no level of degradation from which God cannot redeem. God looks at the rags of humanity with eyes of endearment, "I led them with ..... bonds of love." (11:4) Hosea ends his prophecy with a vision of deliverance. "I will heal their apostasy; I will love them freely." (14:4) When we have sinned, we often are so badly disappointed with ourselves we wonder if anyone (including God) could truly love us, and accept us as a lover. We see no value within ourself.

But the message from God is that He valued us enough to sacrifice His own Son to prove that He could love and deliver us from sin and ourselves!

What's In a Name: Isaac
Genesis 21:3, 6

Abraham had walked with God for 25 years before his son Isaac was born. About 10 years into the journey God had given him a promise that he would have a son. When it really dawned on Sarah that the promise would be fulfilled through her, her immediate reaction was to laugh at the incredulous thought, "after I have become old shall I have pleasure, my Lord being old also?" (Gen 18:12). However late things seem to be to us, God delivers on time.

When Sarah laughed, the Lord questioned her reason for laughing. And there are many reasons besides incredulity. Laughter can be for joyous wonder, for defiance, scorn, or ridicule, and for sheer delight. The Lord wanted to make sure it was not the laughter of unbelief, and countered with, "Is anything too difficult for the Lord?" (See Gen 18:13–14)

God designed us with the ability to laugh, and laughter is part of any whole personality. There seem to be many life situations were laughter is lost. If a person gets sick or is in pain, laughter can evaporate. A major factor in today's world for the loss of laughter is stress. Economic, relational, or psychological pressures drive our laughter away. Still others lose their laughter due to boredom; life gets stuck in a rut. (A rut has been defined as a grave with the ends kicked out.) Sarah, who saw herself as old, found that laughter declined with age. People who refuse to lose their laughter age much slower! An old adage reminds us that "people don't quit laughing because they get old; they get old because they quit laughing." It's still true today!

So I don't find it too unusual for Abraham and Sarah to respond to the birth of their only son with laughter. And that's exactly what they named him, because Isaac means laughter. There's nothing like a baby to rearrange our whole life even when we were young. But to a 90-year-old woman? I think we would all laugh. It's a miracle; it's downright amazing; it's a joy so big it should be shared.

Laughter is one of the greatest reactions we can have. It is a stress reliever. It can calm the tensions in fractured relationships. Laughter helps you digest your food. Laughter helps your mind and body heal. It is with laughter that you learn the best and the most. We tend to remember a good and hearty laugh. Laughter is often associated with the epiphanies or mental breakthroughs. Laughter is also associated with faith, because believing God means we often laugh at impossible situations.

When Isaac was born, "Sarah said, God has made laughter for me: everyone who hears will laugh with me." (21:6) When we laugh, we make our world to be inclusive. Others, not only are invited in, they feel welcomed. When something as big as an Isaac birth happens, we have more than enough to share. Laughter and generosity seem to be wed together. I've been in enough homes to know that homes without a good amount of laughter need help. The same is true about churches. Regardless of the cause for the sorrow or sadness, God has a cure. We need a promise from God.

Gestation times for promises aren't always the same, but when our Isaac is born, we can share the laughter with the whole world!

What's In a Name: Isaiah
Isaiah 1:1

In the late 1940's an inquisitive shepherd boy stumbled onto the Qumran caves off the northwest corner of the Dead Sea. The discovery of many parchments and fragments startled the religious sector. Among the various writings was the complete book of Isaiah, a significant boost to both its significance and authenticity. The nation of Israel would later build a museum, the Shrine of the Book, in Tel Aviv, in a fitting honor to the prophet.

Isaiah was a prominent seer, whose ministry spanned the reigns of four kings: Uzziah, Jotham, Ahaz, and Hezekiah. Isaiah is mentioned prominently in the history records of 2 Kings and 2 Chronicles. The name Isaiah means "God has saved." Isaiah's prophetic utterances to the Israelites confronting their sin frequently reminded them that it was only God who has the ability to save them. In the midst of dire warnings Isaiah gives hope by foretelling of the coming Messiah. The virgin birth is prophesied in Is 7:14 and specifically designated the incarnation by naming Him, Immanuel, or "God is with us" in the flesh.

Isaiah then blesses us with another Messianic promise of salvation which is quoted in Matt 4:14-16 and describes Jesus as the light. (Is 9:2) That passage in Isaiah goes on to list names for the Messiah such as "Wonderful, Counselor, Mighty God, Eternal Father, and Prince of Peace." All of these designations point to God saving His people with justice and righteousness. (Is 9:6-7)

Although Moses is referred to more often in the New Testament than Isaiah, Isaiah is the most quoted one, at least 15 times. This is a major validation of the New Testament, as well as confirming Jesus as the Messiah. As a point of literary trivia, 2 Kings 19 and Isaiah 37 are virtually verbatim writings, thus interlocking Isaiah into the history of Israel.

Isaiah had more interaction with Hezekiah than any other monarch. When Sennacherib, King of Assyria, threatened Jerusalem Hezekiah panicked and sent for Isaiah. Hezekiah asked him to pray, but Isaiah was way ahead. He sent the messengers back to the king, "Don't be afraid" because God would once again save the nation. (Is 37:6) The historical records confirm the biblical ones. Isaiah's most significant revelation of the Messiah is found in chapter 53, presenting a "suffering servant." The Jewish mindset was not prepared to see a Savior in either a suffering or servant role. But Paul, in his discourse on Israel's relationship to God, quotes liberally from Isaiah (Rm 9:27-29, 33; 10:16, 20) in his proclamation of salvation to the Jews. Isaiah is quoted in all four of the gospels and in Acts.

There are always significant ironies in the journeys God maps out for his saints. Isaiah's message, time and again, speaks of God saving various people and the nation. He lived up to his name, but in the end we have a twist. Secular history records that Isaiah was executed by a subsequent king, Manasseh, in a most cruel manner. He was stuffed into a log and then they sawed the log in two. There is a reference to that in the Hall of Faith. (Heb 11:37)

God always has the last word and "God has saved" Isaiah, even though they destroyed his body.

What's In a Name: Israel
Genesis 32:28

The first recorded set of twins in scripture was the sons of Isaac and Rebekah. Having been married for many years before the sons were born, they still had not picked out names ahead of time. Rebekah was in obvious discomfort during the pregnancy and could feel the boys struggling within her womb. God revealed to her that "two nations are in your womb; and two peoples shall be separated from your body." (Gen 25:23) Apparently they were only fraternal twins because they were nothing alike. The older was a "rough and rugged" looking baby and was named Esau because of his looks. The second son grabbed the heel of the first and was born that way. That must have been the distinguishing feature and they named him Jacob, or "heel catcher," which in Hebrew understanding meant "supplanter or deceiver." Both boys lived up to their names.

While much of the details of growing up together are abbreviated, two major events are recorded. One occurs not long after the boys became men and Esau had gone out hunting and returned famished. Ever the opportunist, Jacob had cooked a stew and the aroma was tantalizing to hungry Esau. When Esau asked for a bowl of the stew, the brotherly thing would have been to have graciously given him some. But Jacob, sensing the desperation and weakness of character in Esau, offered to exchange it for his birthright. What had been conferred upon him because he was born a minute or two earlier was flittered away in this moment. (Gen 25:29-34)

Giving blessing to the children was a Hebrew tradition, but the greatest blessing was reserved for the oldest son. With assistance from his mother, Jacob deceived his father and was given the blessing reserved for Esau. When Esau became aware of Jacob's deception, he exclaimed "Is he not rightly named Jacob, for he has supplanted (taken by treachery) me these two times?" (27:36) When Jacob was with his uncle Laban, he was challenged by him and his deceitful ways. Even then Jacob was able to out deceive his uncle.

After twenty years, in that combative situation, Jacob was ready to go home and face his misdeeds. While Jacob was fearful of his brother's wrath, his bigger challenge, as with all of us, is to face ourselves. We must then allow God to fully reveal our own heart. For Jacob, this occurred at a private audience with God at Peniel. He wrestled with a man who was head on with his question, "What is your name?" (32:27) That question is tantamount to saying, "what is your character?" Jacob did not dodge the question when he responded, "Jacob" (deceiver). In that moment, God transformed Jacob's character and renamed him, "Israel." This encounter with God wasn't a feel good session. "I have seen God face to face" was a declaration of God's grace effecting cleansing in his evil nature. God memorialized this event with changing Jacob's name to Israel, which meant someone who could prevail with the Almighty.

Jacob's past deceit was incompatible with the holiness of God. The God of Abraham and Isaac had now become the God of Jacob as well. God's work can survive the passing of generations when each descendant moves into personal contact with the Almighty. It wasn't a matter of carrying on an identity as a Jew, but claiming true faith for one's self. The God of Jacob had become God in Jacob, a man named Israel.

What's In a Name: Jabez
1 Chronicles 4:9 – 10

In the inspired Word we are sometimes given parenthetical expressions, even stories that seemed to have no antecedent foundation and no subsequent reference. The story of Jabez is one of them and his prayer recorded in 1 Chronicles 4:10 has been the subject of some excellent writings such as "The Prayer of Jabez" by Bruce Wilkerson. Why God chose the story to be included we don't know, but it has an interesting principle.

The reading of verse nine suggests that Jabez's mother had a very painful experience with his birth. Since all births have pain associated with them, this must've been a very grievous experience. Even when birth experiences are unpleasant, few mothers would memorialize the event in the naming of the child. That seems to be exactly what happened "because I bore him with pain" was the justification for naming him Jabez which means "pain, grief, or sorrow." Can you imagine being reminded of the grief you caused your mother every time someone spoke your name – dozens of times each day! I'm sure modern psychologists would have evaluated the resulting negative self-image to be fully justified and the only solution would be to change his name! Had Jabez turned out to be a rascal, a misfit in society, the blame would've been placed on his mother. "Look what she did to him." "With a name like pain, what do you expect?" "If he is a pain in the neck, he's just living up to his name."

Regardless of what moniker with which you've been saddled, we all have the power of choice. We can choose to accept God's grace in our life and live above the expectations. So many don't live up to a good name that we conclude that is the norm. But the text clearly states that Jabez was more honorable than his brothers. Whether his name was used as a positive motivation or not is an assumption on our part.

I can hear friends and neighbors asking his mother, "What were you thinking?" The term honorable in Jewish understanding meant "to carry weight" or to garner a higher respect. The basis for honor is godly character and his character must have been observable. Great deeds usually stem from character and godly character is gained by correctly responding to the troubles in our life. When people called His name, it was a reminder to pray. When it says he called on God's name, he was in earnest; he addressed God by name; he accosted him. The context suggested he was focused and insistent when he prayed (in contrast to his unnamed brothers).

He prayed a prayer that had not only had great expectations; it had a bit of irony, too. "Keep me from harm, that it may not pain (grief) me." Jabez took what some would have considered a huge obstacle to success and turned it to his advantage. When God answered in such a resounding way, people forgot that Jabez meant pain because now it was associated with abundance.

We have names given to us by parents, friends, or enemies. Sometimes they're given to us in derision: loser, naïve, unredeemable, sinner, convict, etc. But when we respond by calling on His name, our lives can be blessed and enlarged. Names are never a limitation to the power of God.

Sometimes God may change a name, but more often grace-power simply changes what a name means. Only God knows what's in a name!

What's In a Name: Jeremiah
Jeremiah 1:1

Jeremiah, whose prophetic utterance in the Old Testament is the longest book other than Psalms, was a prophet for over forty years. His service to the nations of Israel covered the last five kings. He witnessed the exile to Babylon although he was given the option not to go. When Jeremiah was just a youth, God revealed His call to him, "Before I formed you in the womb I knew you, and before you were born I consecrated you; I have appointed you a prophet to the nations." (Jer 1:5) While every preacher has a difficult task to confront people with their sin, Jeremiah's job was extra tough. The Israelites were constantly turning away from God to worship idols. In spite of Jeremiah's dire warnings of impending destruction, the people persisted and received the prophesied troubles.

It's quite clear Jeremiah did not volunteer his service. God anticipated some of Jeremiah's reluctance when He told him, "Do not say, 'I am a youth.'" (v 7) God reached out and touched his mouth and told him, "I have put My words into your mouth." (v 9)

Since Jeremiah came from a priestly family in Anathoth, a Levite town on the outskirts of Jerusalem, it is not unusual for his name to have a "God" component. His name means "God will rise." His parents obviously named him with hope in mind. Based on the deteriorating circumstances during those final kings, Jeremiah would need hope to keep his own equilibrium.

The obstinate response Jeremiah so often received caused so many tears, he is known as the "weeping prophet." (9:1) Jeremiah had to contend with a bevy of false prophets who predicted peace and prosperity while he was warning of doom and destruction. These false prophets had "healed the brokenness of My people superficially, saying, 'Peace, peace,' but there is no peace." (6:14) The sinfulness was so engrained they were no longer embarrassed by the shame, just as it is in our generation. "They did not even know how to blush." (6:15)

In the midst of all the messages of woe that Jeremiah had to deliver, he was given some Messianic hope. He was able to see the "righteous Branch" who would do justice and righteousness." (23:5) In the meantime he had to fight for his life. After preaching "in the house of the Lord" (26:7) the priests, prophets, and people seized him saying, "You must die!" (v 8) Have any of you pastors received such a reaction after you have preached?

Even though the message of certain captivity was his burden, he was also the one to prophesy deliverance in 70 years. It happened exactly as he predicted. Jeremiah was faithful to deliver God's messages even when it cost him his freedom. He was imprisoned more than once, and had a horrible experience of being thrown into an old cistern where he sunk deep into the mire. Fortunately, God rescued him before death would come.

Even though his subsequent book, Lamentations, is filled with sorrow, woe and even despair, in the middle Jeremiah affirms the meaning of his name, God will rise, with this perspective from his writing.

"The Lord's loving kindnesses indeed never cease, His compassions never fail, they are new every morning; great is Thy faithfulness." (Lam 3:22-23)

What's In a Name: Jezebel
1 Kings 16:31

There is a long-standing debate on whom has the most influence in the spiritual direction of a family: husband or wife. There is a powerful illustration in the Old Testament. Ahab became king of Israel and had already determined to do evil. He is described as one who "did evil in the sight of the Lord more than all who were before him." (1 Kings 16:30). With that as his stage, "though it had been a trivial thing for him to walk in the sins of Jereboam.... he married Jezebel the daughter of Ethbaal, the King of the Sidonians." (v 31)

To understand this connection we must examine the religious worship of the Sidonians. While they were one of many nations that promoted Baal, their main attraction was the goddess, Asherah. Asherah symbolized sexual passion and immorality was a part of their worship. So I find it interesting that the king of the Sidonians would name his daughter, Jezebel. The original meaning of the name is "chaste." We don't know if the parents equated the name with the prevailing standard of conduct or they wished something better than the norm.

Here's one of the most extreme examples of a life lived completely contrary to her name's meaning. It was so dramatic that she redefined the understanding. Ask anyone today what Jezebel means and they will tell you a loose woman, a prostitute, a floozy, or some other description of one with evil character. It carried such a bad connotation that I have never known parents to name a daughter, Jezebel in the thousands of years since that time.

Once Jezebel married Ahab she seems to have usurped the power from her husband to do whatever she pleased. The prophet Elijah was a thorn in the side of Jezebel and but for his confrontation and restraint, she may have been far worse. Earlier on, she had "the prophets of the Lord" killed. (1Kings 18:13). In their place she promoted the prophets of Baal and Asherah. Much to Jezebel's chagrin, Elijah sent a challenge and 850 prophets, "who eat at Jezebel's table" were confronted on Mount Carmel and lost! When informed, Jezebel sent a 24-hour death threat to Elijah. Had he not fled the scene, she surely would have had him executed.

The next display of her brazen sin occurred when she learned Ahab wanted a certain vineyard. Ahab had tried to buy it and when Naboth refused, he went home and pouted. Ever the schemer, Jezebel set up a plot to steal it. By setting up false witnesses, she had Naboth, a righteous man, condemned and executed. That enabled Ahab to take possession free, but a great spiritual price. (2 Kings 21:16, 19). Ahab is described as one for whom "there was no like" and "sold himself to do evil in the sight of the Lord, because Jezebel his wife incited him. " (21:25) Jezebel's wickedness did not stop with the death of Ahab. She became the primary influencer for their son, Jehoram,, who became King. Even late in life she is known by "the harlotries of your mother Jezebel and her witchcrafts are so many." (2 Kings 9:22) The influence was still known in New Testament times. It may have been a symbolic name for a woman in the church at Thyatira, but this self-labeled prophetess was leading many astray into sexual sins. (Rev 2:20).

The ideal of "chaste" is contrasted by just one woman who was so deep in sinfulness that the name Jezebel lives on in infamy.

What's In a Name: Job
Job 1:1

One of the colorful characters of the Old Testament was Job. Some scholars regard the book of Job as the oldest written literature of the Bible. We are simply introduced to the saga with the words "there was a man." The "land of Uz" means the place of consultation. Whether Job was one to consult with others or he was the one that people consulted is not detailed for us. Nevertheless, he is the central figure of the entire book.

Job's prominence seems to stem from both his character and his wealth. Described in various translations as "perfect, blameless, or upright," Job's integrity seems to be well known and unquestioned. It is rather refreshing to see this quality of character in conjunction with great wealth, a rarity in our world even among professing Christians.

As the story unfolds, we observe a conversation between God and Satan. The meeting was on a day when "the sons of God" presented themselves and Satan seemed to be an uninvited guest. God sees him and confronts him about Job. Of course, God knew Satan had been eyeing him and wanted very much to attack him. But Satan had not been able to penetrate the "hedge of protection" that God had erected.

The name Job means "hated or persecuted" and Satan seemed determined to make his name a reality in his life. Job certainly had not allowed that name to be a detriment to success in material wealth or in his relationship to God. Satan, as the "accuser of the brethren" (Lev 12:10) suggests that Job's faithfulness to God was bought with blessings. Too often we serve Christ just for the perceived benefits.

There are many who stumble in their faith and commitment to God when difficulties come. Trouble never causes unbelief or weakness in character; it only exposes it! Examine the "heroes of faith" and we quickly discover the depth of suffering that defined their moral strength. Each of the saints emerged from suffering with stronger faith and resolve.

Satan was given permission to destroy Job's possessions and subsequently to destroy his health. While most people's health and wealth are determined by their own choices, others have external circumstances beyond their control. Outside observers cannot always discern the difference. Since we value both, it is a major trial when we have lost a major contributor to our support systems. Job's friends were among those who because of their own bias felt Job's troubles were self-generated. They encouraged Job to repent of whatever hidden sins there were. There are many who see those with difficulties as being punished by God. But those who have that attitude do not have a clear view of God's processes. And some have clouded their understanding because of some guilt they're hiding in their own lives.

We do not know over how many years the book of Job spans. But in the end, God not only vindicates Job, He adds to his wisdom and stature. By whomever he may have been hated or persecuted, it wasn't by Almighty God, and ultimately only God's opinion counts. God doesn't always restore lost wealth, but in this case he doubled it! Although suffering is associated with Job, we generally don't think of him as hated, but pitied. God is the ultimate judge, and provider.
God's gift of grace to Job and his acceptance of it, even in the valley of trouble, brought a noteworthy ending!

What's In a Name: Joel
Joel 1:1

There are a dozen Israelites in the Old Testament named Joel, so that was a popular name. One of those was the prophet, whose name is attached to the book that records his prophetic utterances. It is interesting that there are no men recorded in the New Testament who were named Joel.

Joel was another of the Jewish prophets who seem to appear out of nowhere to deliver a message received directly from God. In a day and age when we wish to authenticate words by human credentialing processes, we should take note that God often used unknown men and women to confront the evils of their day. God is looking for willing and obedient hearts, and He alone can instill the wisdom necessary to carry out difficult assignments. God's criteria for selection of His servants vary greatly from ours.

The name Joel (Hebrew is Yow'el) literally means "Yahweh is God," sometimes interpreted to mean Yahweh (Jehovah) is his God. "Yow" refers to the self-existent eternal God and "El" represents the Almighty. In the developing thought of a pluralistic world view, finding someone who understands his identity and purpose in life is wonderful. Whenever there is a sinful generation, the revelation of God is clouded. We can argue cause and effect. Does the loss of the revelation of God lead to a sinful generation, or does yielding to sin cause the dimming of our view of God? That both seem to be occurring simultaneously is a truism. Joel was called to confront his generation with their sinfulness. Most societies ignore sin until they are forced to live with dire consequences.

In living up to his name, Joel could deliver "the word of the Lord" without any admixture of corruption. He had no personal agenda—he wasn't motivated by any past events and he wasn't trying to manipulate himself into future positions. After all it wasn't his message; he was just the messenger.

Even though sin is repugnant to the essential nature of God, His love, mercy and grace are stronger. God's eternal purpose is the redemption of mankind. God doesn't primarily work through organizations and systems. He works through dedicated individuals. This prophet Joel, with no prior history of religious service, is suddenly the spokesman for God. The communication tool that God uses to prepare people for effective service is divine revelation. As much as we value education today, it alone is insufficient to equip someone for results in the Kingdom.

Joel was such a voice for God that he was still the subject of the apostles on the day of Pentecost. "But this is what was spoken by the prophet Joel...." (Acts 2:16 NKJV) Some eight or nine hundred years after Joel delivered God's word, the Holy Spirit was fulfilling that prophecy. Even though Joel had spoken clearly about the sins of Israel, in the true nature of his name, he was also trusted to speak about the outpouring of the Spirit of God which propelled the young church to transform society. That Joel "saw" the future is a testament to his dynamic relationship with Yahweh. When God is revealed through men like Joel, and the Almighty God works through these servants, a legacy of divine power is displayed as it was on the day of Pentecost.

I pray that we will by faith experience another outpouring of the Spirit and live to see the day!

What's In a Name: John
Luke 3:2

While there were several named John in the New Testament, we'll start by looking at John the Baptist. John's father, Zechariah, was a faithful priest and his mother, Elizabeth, was known for her piety. They had been childless after being married for a lengthy time, and in those days that was considered a disgrace, maybe as the result of sinfulness. Zachariah was serving his priestly duties when he was accosted by an angel, who informed him that he and his wife would have a special son born to them. (See Luke 1:11-20)

In that initial interchange with the angel, Zechariah was given an instruction to name this son, John. Tradition would have dictated that he would be named after his father. Zechariah was certainly a good name which meant "Jah (God) has remembered." But this son was to be called John, meaning "favored (beloved) by God." Along with this specific name came a commissioning. "He will also go before Him (Jesus) in the spirit and power of Elijah, 'to turn the hearts of the fathers to the children,' and the disobedient to the wisdom of the just, to make ready a people prepared for the Lord." (Luke 1:17 NKJV)

Young people are always trying to "find themselves" but don't succeed unless they find God's purpose for living. Whatever the assignment we find ourselves doing, we can do it with excellence when we know we are empowered by the Spirit of God. Knowing we are favored by God, gives us confidence in completing our mission, especially when we encounter the problems and difficulties of life. Opposition will surely occur, and victory only comes when we persevere. Trials are given to "make us" not break us.

John the Baptist had need of these inner assurances when Herod became angry with him and put him in prison. He had thrived on being obedient to his calling and saw hundreds come to repentance. No doubt he felt he was seeing his vision fulfilled as the one who prepared the way for the ministry of Jesus Christ. But stuck away in the prison, he had doubts. "And John, calling two of his disciples to him, sent them to Jesus, saying, "Are You the Coming One, or do we look for another?" (Luke 7:19 NKJV)

Jesus did not answer the question directly, but sent the disciples back to John to report on the powerful ministry to the blind, deaf, lepers, poor, lame, and the resurrection of the dead. (See verse 22.) All of us will face a time when we can no longer be in the trenches of spiritual warfare. It is especially difficult when we relish the action and the challenge of winning. We so easily forget the victories won when we are shut away from the affirming crowds. But God does not withdraw His favor or love to us. The legacy of John was welded to the ministry of Jesus and his labors continued to bear fruit. "For the gifts and the calling of God are irrevocable." (Rom 11:29 NKJV) Many of those whose ministries are recorded in scripture were those who only had a short-term assignment. Even though John met an untimely and tragic death (He was beheaded.) we need not doubt that he had fulfilled a special place in the Kingdom. The world grapples with the question, "Who am I?" and finds it difficult to answer. Christians ask a more fundamental and important question, "Whose am I?"

When our relationship is secure in Christ, we all experience the name, John, because we are favored by God!

What's In a Name: Joseph
Genesis 30:24

Although Rachel was the beloved wife of Jacob, she was not a mother. Her frustration was expressed in her plea to her husband, "Give me children, or else I die." Jacob became angry and retorted, "Am I in the place of God?" (See Gen 30:1-2) Later however, "God remembered Rachel" and she was able to conceive. (vv 22-23) When she delivered her son, she named him Joseph, which means "may God add." Her actual comment at the time was "May the Lord give me another son." (v 24) As thrilled as Rachel was about Joseph, she wasn't satisfied with just one. She hardly gave little Joseph time to make his first cry before her thoughts were on having another one. While she was able to realize the goal of having a second son, the birthing process was so difficult she lost her life immediately after knowing she had delivered her son. (Gen 35:17-18)

Other than being a favorite son of his father, nothing seemed to be spectacular until Joseph was seventeen. It was at that time that God began to add to Joseph's life. God had a particular destiny for Joseph and in order to fulfill his mission, Joseph needed significant preparation. The first addition to Joseph was to instill the vision via dreams. The dreams basically told the same message, that Joseph would become a ruler over his family. Since Joseph's relationship with his brothers was already bad, (They hated him. Gen 37:4) his telling them his dreams produced overt antagonism. We can conclude from the context that he related his dreams with an arrogant attitude.

God knew Joseph could not be a ruler with righteousness if he was not developed in his character. To fully understand how to lead one must first learn to follow. My guess is that as Dad's pet, he was protected from the menial jobs assigned to his brothers. He served as a messenger boy for his father but knew very little about serving.   So God allowed him to be sold into slavery. As God added the education gained in this School of Slavery, it seems Joseph was promoted to "personal servant" of Potiphar, the Egyptian officer. (Gen 39:2-4) Joseph's development was still not complete so God added another course, this time in graduate studies. Joseph's sterling character was demonstrated by his rebuff to Potiphar's wife, "How then could I do this great evil, and sin against God?" (Gen 39:9)

But God allowed a false charge to dictate the next few years of Joseph's life, and the charge was in the area in which Joseph had shown stalwart integrity. It may have seemed like God was subtracting from Joseph's life during those years, although there is no biblical record that Joseph ever displayed a bad attitude towards the injustice. God not only fulfilled the dreams given in his youth, God added abundance to it. He married and God blessed with two sons. Then God added his whole family back to him there in Egypt where they could all be provided for with abundance. The story of Joseph ends with a discussion with his brothers following the death of their father. Even though they had brotherly harmony added to their family, the brothers were still fearful of pent-up reprisals. Joseph assured them that God had added heavenly perspective, "what you meant for evil, God meant for good." (Gen 50:20)

When we fulfill our mission from God we become a Joseph: one who adds value to others, and others to the Kingdom.

What's In a Name: Joshua
Exodus 17:9

Many of the biblical characters are abruptly introduced without any background or buildup. Such is the case with Joshua, whose first mention is as a military leader fighting against the Amalekites. It's the first recorded battle following the Exodus. How and where Joshua got his training remains a mystery. (See Ex 17:8 – 13) Our next glimpse of him is as Moses' assistant when he accompanied him "up to the mountain of God." When Moses was speaking with God, and watching God write the Ten Covenant Commands, Joshua seems to be a silent observer.

Since there are no previous persons named Joshua, this is not a name of heritage. His parents would have been stretching the limits in naming their son Joshua, because the name means "Jehovah saves." The Israelites held the name of God so sacred that they would only whisper the name. So to have a variation on the name of God would've been considered sacrilegious by the more conservative ones. The Greek equivalent of Joshua is Jesus, and that name meant the one "who could save people from their sins." (Matt. 1:21). Nun, Joshua's father, welcomed the birth of his son as the captivity in Egypt was drawing to a close. Apparently he had not lost hope in God's ability and willingness to intervene and deliver the Israelites from the oppressive bondage.

Nun himself was given an interesting name because it means "re- sprouting" or perpetual. Recognizing his ability to reproduce his faith and his offspring, he seems to have passed on sterling character and profound faith in Joshua. Perhaps no one in the Old Testament represents a better type of Christ than

Joshua. There is no biblical record of wrongdoing by him. Considering the fact that God was very transparent about the failure of his saints, it is remarkable that no such blunders are recorded. Some persons seem to be born with a specific mission in life. In Joshua's case he may have been aware of it early, and remained committed to it his whole life. Joshua showed himself faithful in each assignment, whether in the military, spiritual assistant, spy, or political leader. One of the greatest illustrations of godly character in leadership was his willingness to be subservient. He was the number two man for 40 years without complaint, jealousy, or ambition to take over. Even when he was elevated to leadership he did not disparage Moses or try to extol his own leadership as being better or more important.

The transition of leadership from Moses to Joshua seemed seamless. Joshua was single-minded in his drive to take the Israelites into the land of Canaan. As focused as he was, he was simply another ante-type of Jesus. Jesus was equally focused on his mission to go to the cross. Each of these men ventured into the enemy's camp with courage to conquer. Joshua had the land and giants to conquer; Jesus had Satan and death to defeat. Joshua never forgot that it is Jehovah who saves and never took the credit to himself for any of the victories. He knew to seek God's plan for each battle, because God's uniqueness and creativity finds another way to win each struggle. Joshua's influence at the end of his life was strong enough to force the question of choosing to serve God or not. (Josh 24:15) His legacy of leadership: "Israel served God all the days of Joshua, and all the days of the elders who survived Joshua." (24:31)

"Jehovah saves" is needed for our generation!

What's In a Name: Malachi
Malachi 1:1

In many arguments, the winner is the one who gets the last word. Not that He needs the final say to win, but God always "seals the deal" in His favor. As a post-script to the Old Testament interaction between Israel and God, God speaks through Malachi. The name means "administrative messenger." It's meant to imply that the messenger comes with the full authority to speak. Whereas a courier service might be hired to deliver information, a decision of eternal proportions would only be entrusted to a trustworthy source. God saw that level of character in Malachi and allowed him to speak for Him in what would be the only voice from God for the next 400 years. That dry spell of revelation would finally be interrupted by the births of John the Baptist and Jesus just six months apart.

So many prophets that God had sent had "preached to deaf ears," just completely ignored. Others faced confrontation and several were jailed. With Malachi, God gave him a unique style. He would make a statement concerning a topic and then pose questions regarding the subject. The answers to the rhetorical questions provide the substance of God's views on many different issues.

One of the fundamental attitudes that Malachi addresses is respect for God. A son is to honor his father and a servant is to respect his master, so Malachi poses the question, "Where is my honor or respect?" He responds with a declaration, "For from the rising of the sun, even to its setting, My name will be great among the nations." (Mal 1:11) Part of the disrespect the priests were showing toward God dealt with blemished offerings (offering less than our best). An even greater deficiency was that priest (ministers) who should have "preserved knowledge" and given godly instruction, "turned aside from the way" and "caused many to stumble" in their corrupt teaching and showing partiality. (Mal 2:7-9)

While Malachi was truly God's messenger for the time, he is prophetically speaking of John the Baptist as an authoritative emissary to cleanse the way for the coming of Christ. (3:1) In response to the question, "who can stand when He appears?" Malachi describes Jesus as a "refiners' fire" or "fuller's (laundryman's) soap." (v 2) Our world clamors for comfort and convenience; God is concerned with cleansing and character. Malachi also addresses the issue of tithing. Truly the management of our money, not just the 10%, is a clear measurement of the spiritual state of our heart. Whether openly or covertly, the 10th Commandment is widely desecrated.

The finale of this prophecy strikes me as the most relevant. If there is any failure of God's people more than to transfer their faith to the next generation, I don't know what it would be. The promise to send the great prophet Elijah was specifically to "restore (turn) the hearts of the fathers to their children, and the hearts of the children to their fathers." (4:6) Failure to do that is described as a curse or ban of destruction. It is interesting that Luke refers to this directive in telling Zecharias that his son's (John the Baptist) mission in life is this precisely. (See Luke 1:17) God's messenger, Malachi, still speaks to our generation that our most important task is the turning of hearts within the family.

Are you listening?

What's In a Name: Mary
Luke 1:27

Perhaps no name in scripture is more well-known than Mary. The most identified person with this name is the mother of Jesus. The gospel writer Luke gives us a little background. "...the angel Gabriel was sent by God to a city of Galilee named Nazareth, to a virgin betrothed to a man whose name was Joseph, of the house of David. The virgin's name was Mary. And having come in, the angel said to her, 'Rejoice, highly favored one, the Lord is with you; blessed are you among women!'" (Luke 1:26-28 NKJV) God does not detail in the record why Mary was chosen from all the virgins in Israel, but God's choice was informed by a personal visit from one of the archangels.

Looking on we might conclude that Mary was a righteous person, had the right personality and disposition, and perhaps other desirable traits. But whatever the reason, the choice was clear and Mary was a willing participant in God's scheme of incarnation. Based on that, we would guess that the meaning of Mary's name was "pure, sweet, saintly or even fruitful." But such is not the case. Based on an old Hebrew word from which the name Miriam is also derived, the meaning is "rebellious or bitter." One of the famous places of defiant rebellion by the Israelites was Marah. (See Ex 15:23-25) Moses sister, Miriam, illustrated her rebellion and bitterness more than once. (For example, see Num 12)

Why would God pick someone whose name means rebellious and bitter to give birth to His Son, knowing that her name would be immortalized in history? Perhaps one explanation is given in the primary theme of scripture: redemption. Before God created the world, He designed the plan of redemption. His plan was so complete that no human could ever be outside the scope of being redeemable. Whether Mary was sweet and kind from childhood, we don't know. But we do know that by the time the angel Gabriel visited her, her heart was immediately responsive to God's call.

Regardless of the origin of names, they seem to take on meanings related to the conduct or disposition of the person. If we know someone who is disgusting, we skip over that name when suggesting names for newborns. Since WWII there have been few who named their sons Adolph. Since Bible times, the name Judas has been studiously avoided. It is ironic that God illustrates salvation through the redemption of names as well as lives.

There were several Mary's in the New Testament and all of them seem to have a redemption story. Two outstanding Mary's with redemptive stories are Mary of Bethany (Lazarus' sister) and Mary Magdalene. Whatever their beginning, the grace and love of Jesus transformed their life so completely that the name Mary no longer has a stigma attached.

Rebellion and bitterness are pictured in scripture as difficult ones for which God must deal. Rebellion is equated with witchcraft. (See 1 Sam 15:23) God has a much different attitude toward failure from weakness, than He does when rebellion is defiant.

But Mary's life gives a real testimony: Redemption triumphs over rebellion!

What's In a Name: Matthew
Matthew 9:9

Matthew was an eyewitness to the ministry of Jesus Christ and it appears his connection to Jesus covered the entire time that Jesus ministered on earth, as well as during the early church years. Although Matthew was a Jew, he had taken on the job of being a tax collector for the Roman government. What background Matthew had in religious studies we don't know. The record only gives us the religious experience of the succinct invitation by Jesus, "Follow me." (Mt 9:9) This encounter occurred, not at some spiritual gathering, but at the tax office.

Matthew's parents not only had a strong belief in God, but they understood that having a child was a privilege granted by God. Matthew simply means "gift of God." Too much of our world has either never known, or has forgotten, God's creative work in conception. Biological processes cannot be attributed to mechanical functions. The psalmist Solomon articulated it well when he wrote, "Behold, children are a heritage (gift) from the LORD, The fruit of the womb is a reward." (Ps 127:3 NKJV)

The sinful society in which we live labels children as a bother, a liability, or worse. Whenever society does not recognize the value God has placed in creation and procreation, the end result is abortion, abuse, and infanticide.

Because of the selfish bent of the current world view, we see little gratitude. It displays itself in our attitudes toward gifts. How do we calculate the value of a gift? It is usually not in the amount of money expended. Rather it begins with our concept of the position and power of the giver. If the person who donates to us is of great importance, we tend to value the gift more, though do we not understand it all. More important than our view of the donor's reputation is our relationship with that person. The more we sense we are loved and valued, the more we value the gift.

Other considerations will also be in the thoughtfulness of the giver. When it is obvious that the person understood our needs or desires and met or exceeded those expectations, the greater value we perceive the gift to be. Sometimes we are awed with the presentation of the gift both in appearance or circumstances. When parents see a child as a special gift from God, it changes the entire perspective for both parents and children. What we value, we invest in and protect. We tend to express and repeat our gratitude.

Our mindset always frames our attitudes, and is reflected in our speech. Children do not generally do what we tell them to do; rather they do what they see us doing. They quickly absorb our attitudes. They simply live out what is spoken to them. If we say, "You never do anything right," they often quit trying to do what is right. If our words are always condemning what they do, they reflect that condemning spirit in their own relationships.

When we value the Giver, we will value the gift. When we value the gift, we focus not on what's lacking, but on what's useful and good. Jesus demonstrated his love (value) of us in that "while we were yet sinners" (Rm 5:8) He gave His life. Every child is a "gift from God." Matthew stands out as an example.

Give thanks today to God, your parents, and your children. You are highly valued!

What's In a Name: Micah
Micah 1:1

Micah was another Jewish prophet primarily to the tribe of Judah. He followed Amos by a few years, but the circumstances had not changed so his message is remarkably similar. He denounced the ethical sins and the social situation of the rich oppressing the poor. The religious and judicial leaders were corrupt, and attempts to call them to account were dismissed. This prophecy illustrates that sin has the same effect on society no matter the time in history.

As with other prophets, Micah was able to interlace his warnings and prophesies of doom with prophecies of promise. In this case he prophesied the birth of the Messiah in Bethlehem. (See Micah 5:2) It is simply amazing that no matter how dark the days seem, God always keeps the hope of redemption alive. He interlaces the dark night of hopelessness with rays of hope!

The name Micah means "Who is like God?" Another name derived from the same Hebrew root word is Michael, and so has the same meaning. His name in itself is a constant reminder that we are to compare society to a holy God, and not to ourselves. So many, and Christians included, simply view the rest of the world from their own self-centered image. God is often forgotten as we counter the "Me too" and especially the "Me first" generations.

Micah's prophecy is a classical statement which sums up the height of Old Testament Religion. "He has shown you, O man, what is good; And what does the LORD require of you, But to do justly, To love mercy, And to walk humbly with your God?"

(Mic 6:8 NKJV) This is an expanded version of the question in his name, "Who is like God?" In this verse he explains that those who are striving to be like God will first of all be justice-minded. The verb "do" in the Hebrew is comprehensive meaning not just to try but to accomplish or to complete acts of justice. The typical response of our culture is to look away. Getting involved requires too much commitment, getting our hands dirty, and aligning ourselves with undesirable people. (Of course, Jesus did just that!)

The second criterion given was to love mercy. The Hebrew word is primarily not one of pity, but of kindness. Doing acts of kindness is insufficient for a Christian; it must be done with a love for the work and the recipient. (Again, Jesus is a great example!) Kindness erupts into action from a foundation of a kind heart.

The final comparison is to "walk humbly." Pride prevents us from doing a lot of things Christ would normally do. Humility is not putting ourselves down, but rather lifting others up. The Hebrew word even indicates accepting humiliation if it advances the Kingdom of God and helps others. Pride is not only the first sin, it is also foundational to most other sins. The sin of pride always creates a fracturing of relationships. Church groups have been famous for creating criteria niches for accepting others. But preachers of the Word will constantly remind us of "Who is like God?" When I take this as a personal inventory and compare myself to God, I am always praying for mercy! Micah not only witnessed faithfully to his generation, his words are a constant reminder that in the judgment, we will only be confronted with "are you like God?"

We need Micah to speak to our generation!

What's In a Name: Miriam
Numbers 12:1

Miriam first appears on the biblical scene as an unnamed older sister with a specific assignment. Her baby brother of three months has been placed in a basket in the Nile River and she stands back and watches to see what will happen. (See 2:4) When Pharoah's daughter saw the little bundle, and her heart was touched, big sister rushed over and suggested that a Hebrew mother would be ideal as a surrogate. So Jochebed reared her own son for the first few years.

Miriam reappears in the biblical record following the crossing of the Red Sea. Moses had directed the special appearance of the "Sons of Israel" choir. (Ex 15:1-19) Not to be outdone, Miriam, now a prophetess, assembled the women and sang a response. (vv 20-21) Even though these first two appearances contributed something positive, it appears that Miriam had issues. She was lurking in the shadows as she watched this baby brother achieve both national and international fame.

The name Miriam means "rebellious" and that rebellion seems to stem from bitterness. Often the surface seems to be calm, but underneath is the "streak of wildness." In the next glimpse we have of Miriam this nature is revealed. "Then Miriam and Aaron spoke against (criticized) Moses because of the Cushite woman whom he had married." (Num 12:1) Why that was an issue with Miriam we are not told. It's obvious from the context even though both Miriam and Aaron were involved, Miriam was the instigator. She was mentioned first; she received the punishment (v 10) and Aaron had shown himself to be easily manipulated by others. [Ex 32:1-6]

Miriam had never been officially appointed to anything by Moses or by a divine directive. She was self-appointed and saw her role as keeping Moses straight. She may have seen herself as the guardian stemming from the original assignment of watching out for baby Moses. Though Moses showed an arrogant attitude during the first third of his life, following the Exodus he is described as "very humble, more than any man who was on the face of the earth." (Num 12:3) So Miriam's outburst was her own internal struggle erupting to the surface. And Moses made no attempt to defend his actions; but God intervened.

God's scolding of Miriam and Aaron leaves no room for them to question Moses' leadership. This illustrates that self-appointed guardians of the "orthodoxy" often reveal their own character flaws when they try to manufacture reasons to criticize. Even though the leprosy she contracted appears to have been healed the same day, she was forced to endure the indignity of being "shut up outside the camp for seven days." (v 15)

Her death is one of the very few deaths of females recorded in scripture, thus giving her some prominence. (Num 20:1) But it might be recorded for another reason. "Remember what the Lord your God did to Miriam on the way as you came out of Egypt." (Dt 24:9) In other words, God is using her story as a reminder to us that any streak of rebellion needs to be cleansed from our natures. It takes a divine work. We knew her name was never changed. Grace would have kept the root of bitterness from springing up again. Her name did not cause a rebellious heart, but it seems to have revealed it.

When grace invades a heart even the contrary can become delightedly obedient.

What's In a Name: Moses
Exodus 2:10

It would be easy to call the start of Moses' life a dramatic beginning. His parents were faced with an edict from Pharaoh: "every son who is born, you are to cast into the Nile." (Ex 1:22). So Moses' parents did comply with the rule, just three months late. His mother waterproofed a basket and harbored it in the reeds so it wouldn't float out to sea. His older sister was stationed nearby to keep watch over the baby. (Ex 2:4)

In God's providence it was Pharaoh's daughter who discovered the basket and sent her maid to retrieve it. Touched by the pitiful cry of the baby, she made an on-the-spot decision to adopt him. He was given the name Moses to commemorate his sensational rescue, meaning "drawn out of the water" or in the larger context, rescued. So Moses began life as the world's first "basket case." The book of Exodus centers on the life of Moses as he is mentioned by name in 31 of the 40 chapters.

The defining word in Moses' life is the word rescue. Either he needed to be rescued, or he was working to rescue someone else. The first major encounter recorded as an adult was Moses attempting to rescue a Hebrew brother from a beating by an Egyptian task master. His unrestrained anger resulted in the death of the Egyptian and caused Moses to flee to the land of the Midianites. There he found the daughters of Reuel mistreated by other shepherds as they tried to water their sheep. (Ex 2:16–17). Once again Moses' instincts kicked in and he rescued them. That rescue was rewarded with a place to live, and one of those seven daughters became his wife. (v 21)

The biblical record skips a few years before we find the burning bush encounter where God calls Moses to lead the most fantastic rescue in human history. This would not be a SWAT team surgically extracting a captive or two in some stealthy escapade. This would involve the movement of some 2 million people with full disclosure. No reporter would be able to scoop the story.

The buildup to the Exodus was layered with 10 plagues that were witnessed by the entire nation. Walking out of the land of Egypt was only the beginning of the rescues. Very quickly they were faced with the Red Sea in front of them. The Egyptian army moved in behind, blocking any retreat or other escape routes. Moses remained the point person to keep the Divine Rescuer on the scene, and the Red Sea divided only long enough for the Israelites to pass. The ingenuity of God is always worth an intensive look. How did God provide the strong east wind that blew two directions at once parting the waters? He blew his nose! (See Exodus 15:8).

The next 40 years simply elongate the story of the rescues. Rescued from starvation by the daily supply of manna, no one could figure out what it was, much less where it came from. This was the original home delivery service. (Ex 16). When thirsty, God rescued them with water from a rock. (Ex 17). Moses was a child of destiny when it came to rescues. However, dramatic beginnings cannot substitute for a life of obedience. God is certainly willing to rescue us from bad circumstances if we'll let him save us from ourselves.

Fulfilling God's mission for us will always involve the rescue of someone else. Go Moses!

What's in the name: Nabal
1 Samuel 25:25

In the world in which we live riches and righteousness are generally considered far apart. Those who become rich have often manipulated information or systems for their own advantage. While it is certainly not necessary, riches and godly character rarely reside within the same person.

In one of the narratives regarding King David we are introduced to an unsavory character named Nabal. Nabal is a businessman who is described as very rich. One measure of his wealth was 3000 sheep and 1000 goats. Since David was hanging out in a nearby wilderness, and because his ragtag army was serving the public by protecting them against roving bandits, David sent him men to ask for provisions. Knowing the circumstances, David thought that just a bit of gratitude would result in generosity. Instead, when the young man asked for help, Nabal was surly and demeaning. "Who is David?" was his question meaning "Who does David think he is?"

What I find really intriguing about this story is the meaning of the name Nabal. The name is synonymous with fool, dolt, or stupid in a wicked way. Whether anyone was ever named that before or since is unknown to me. But to name a son fool in an age when names were to hold significance is an enigma. Why would a mother do that to a child? Was she setting the course of his life, sort of prophetic, or was she angry with herself or God? It becomes rather obvious that he had no trouble living up to his name!

We typically think of a fool is one who lacks good sense, one who shows no wisdom in his decisions or actions Nabal is certainly an example of one who reacts to a situation without considering the consequences. He had little regard for his wife, Abigail, whose name means "source of joy." The scriptural record describes her as "intelligent and beautiful" (1 Sam 25:3) as well as discerning (v 33). Nabal folly cost him both his life and his wife. Abigail refers to her husband as a "son of the Belial" (v 25) meaning a worthless person. Great intelligence, riches, fame, and anything else the world values cannot save a person from stupidity or foolishness. Remember the adage, "stupid is as stupid does."

There are many scriptures that define "fool." Saul allowed jealousy to overcome reason. (1 Sam 26:21) Abner was not alert to whom was a danger to him. (2 Sam 3:33) Proverbs equates fool with one enticed by a harlot (7:22); one who babbles (10:8); one who is right in his own eyes (12:15); one who spreads folly (13:16) or one who repeats a folly. (26:11) Ecclesiastes adds a couple other designations: one who multiplies words (talks too much) (10:14) and one who folds his hands (is lazy). (4:5) Jesus did not want us to indiscriminately call someone a fool (Matt 5:22) but He relates the story of God calling a rich man "fool." (Luke 12:20) His foolish act was an upside down value judgment, i. e., he worried about bigger barns when he was unprepared for heaven. Paul gives us a great instruction, "be careful how you walk, not as fools, but as wise." (Eph 5:15) Nabal lived up to his name and self-destructed. None of us needs to live as fools, silly, stupid or worthless lives. God always provides meaning and mission for each person's life's journey.

God can change your character and your name if you ask for wisdom. See James 1:5.

What's In a Name: Nahum
Nahum 1:1

As with many of the minor prophets Nahum appears on the scene, delivers his singular message, and passes on. The focus of his prophecy is Assyria, a powerful military state. Jonah had been called to deliver a message of repentance about a century and a half earlier. At that time, it seems the whole city did repent and turn to God.

But repentance is not an "event" that lasts in and of itself. Seeking God always requires an element of repenting, which necessitates us surrendering our pride. Individuals, churches and nations all need times of revival and renewal, and those times always start with repenting. (2 Chr 7:14)

People, churches, and countries do not sustain their times of spiritual growth. To meet that challenge, times of revival, renewal, or refreshing are scheduled so that spiritual vitality can be reasserted. God usually begins beckoning us with tender words of compassion. When those overtures of mercy are rejected God often resorts to warnings, even to the point of sounding harsh and vengeful.

The Israelites had their own issues with faithfulness to God. Like so many they looked around at neighboring countries and found others more wicked than themselves. Assyria seemed to be the worst of the lot. It was a little confusing to the Jews that the most wicked country would also be the strongest militarily and the wealthiest. So they cried out, "Has God forsaken Judah? Why do the Assyrians, so full of evil, prosper while we are suffering? Are God's promises empty?"

While Nahum did not answer the questions directly, he gave an astonishing prophecy: Nineveh will fall, and God will save His people. Nahum reminds us "the Lord is slow to anger," (Nah 1:8) but "great in power." As the prophet details the ways God can show His power, we become aware of the justice of the Almighty who "will by no means leave the guilty unpunished." (1:3) The wrath of God is too awesome to ignore. Students of history find this fact compelling.

The name Nahum means "consolation" or "full of comfort." Even while Nahum is delivering the message (burden) imposed on his heart, God is still the God of love, mercy and redemption. The complete ruin of Nineveh and Assyria came about eight years after this prophecy and seemed impossible at the time. "All the nations who forget God" (Ps 9:17) will come to a destructive end no matter how much political might or material wealth they have accumulated.

We should take great comfort in the knowledge of the "end of the story," Even righteous people often suffer great affliction. "For the Lord will restore the splendor of Jacob…even though devastators have devastated them." (2:2) When God restores, it is not a difficult matter for Him to make ruins a monument to history.

God can take people and nations alike and embed His gory. In fact, He delights in taking impossible situations and the things man has rejected to show the depth and power of redemption. Nahum's message may not have been lengthy, but it was powerful. In a world that looks more and more hopeless, it is great to see God still sanctioning comfort.

All those who truly trust Him will not be disappointed.

What's In a Name: Nehemiah
Nehemiah 1:1

God uses all types of persons in His kingdom, including varied personalities in leadership. One of the quality leaders was Nehemiah. His skill and trustworthiness had been noticed and he was appointed as the king's cupbearer. (Neh 1:1) Even though the official captivity of Israel had ended when King Cyrus made his decree, the movement of Jews back to Judea was slow. About eighty years had passed, and Artaxerxes was in his 20th year when Nehemiah learned the plight of Jerusalem.

Nehemiah was an emotional man by nature and when he was informed of the sad state of affairs in Jerusalem, he "sat down and wept and mourned for days; and was fasting and praying before the God of heaven." (Neh 1:4) He was not one who could or would hide his sorrow. Even though he performed his work with excellence the king noticed the difference on his face. "The king said to me, 'why is your face sad though you are not sick? This is nothing but sadness of heart.'" (Neh 2:2)

The name Nehemiah means "the consolation of Jah (God) or God comforts." To console means to give hope, comfort or encouragement in the face of grief, sense of loss, or trouble. Nehemiah moves right into the role naturally and persuades the king to give him a leave of absence to go to Jerusalem. He needed to see first-hand how big a task it would be to rebuild the walls of the city. Even though he had authorization to do the work and all the resources pledged, he understood that motivation would be a greater issue, as it usually is. He began with an inclusive imperative, "Let us arise and build." (2:18) He received an immediate response, "So they put their hands to the good work."

Whenever God is moving, you can be sure Satan will be opposing. In this case the opposition was led by Sanballat, the governor from Samaria. While Jerusalem was leaderless, Sanballat had assumed authority over that city and didn't want to relinquish it. The biblical narrative gives us the systematic way in which Nehemiah gave oversight to the task of rebuilding.

Sanballat and company did not come with military might to stop the work. Rather he resorted to ridicule and discouraging statements. "What are these feeble Jews doing?" "Can they revive the stone from the dusty rubble?" (4:2) Nehemiah responded to the plot with immediate defense measures such as 24 hour guards, especially in the "exposed places" and added a guard in every house. (4:3)

We can see the persistency of Satan when Sanballat tried time and time again to talk, but each time Nehemiah rebuffed them with "I am doing a great work and I cannot come down. Why should the work stop while I leave it and come down to you?" (6:3) For people looking on, having someone consistently stand the test of life is encouraging.

Nehemiah knew that the biggest obstacle to completing a project is discouragement. (6:9) He prayed for God to strengthen his hands. Even though the project was completed in only 52 days (6:15) they had to overcome the negativity at the half-way point. Had Nehemiah not been there to remind them of the vision and God's miraculous help ("Our God will fight for us." 4:20) the project may have been another twenty years for completion.

Praise God for the Nehemiahs who surround us with comfort!

What's In a Name: Nicolas
Acts 6:5

One of the most recognizable corporate logos of our day is the "swish" symbol for Nike. The company name comes from the Greek word nike, and is the name for the goddess of victory. Literally, it is "the means of success." Since one of the cultural values of our age is "success" it's no wonder that Nike has been successful around the world.

Contrast the corporate mindset with the spiritual thinking of our day. When Jesus came to this earth it was not to affirm the religious leaders of that day. His was a message of salvation that He was introducing through the Kingdom of God, which was available to everyone. This Kingdom was unlike the kingdoms of this world in most ways. But like others, a kingdom can only continue to exist if it is victorious in the battles in which it is engaged.

Philosophically, the general thinking of many theologians and pastors is that living a victorious life is a simply an ideal. No matter how hard a Christian tries, they believe that human nature is not fully redeemable. In times past, there was a sense that "clergy" perhaps could live a spiritual life, but many failures of ministers and the public announcements via all the news sources have shattered that myth.

In the early church, we are all familiar with the apostles and that the Holy Spirit worked through them. We are also familiar with a problem that developed in the early church regarding the care of widows. In dealing with that crisis, the church appointed seven laymen to oversee this work. The most prominent of those seven deacons was Stephen. But all of them were "men of good reputation, full of the Spirit and of wisdom." (Acts 6:3) Two of the deacons were Nicanor and Nicolas. (Acts 6:5) Both names are derived from the same root word and mean "victorious" or "conquest."

One of the saddest commentary on a life is for one to be able to conquer the world, but unable to master himself. Nicolas' ability to be victorious in his personal life is directly proportional to his being "full of the Spirit and wisdom." God has an immeasurable reservoir of grace available for us. When God controls our life, we are able to accept that grace, which is the enabling power of God. None of us possesses the strength within ourselves to overcome sin, our weaknesses, and propensities to self-interest.

While we are not given any other insight into the life of Nicolas, we conclude that his life was one of victorious character. The lack of any further complaints is a testimony to the success. To be able to serve cheerfully without contamination in the midst of a complaining world requires more grace than most people possess.

God did not intend to leave us weak or with barely enough strength to carry out the Great Commission. "Where sin abounded, grace did much more abound." (Rom 5:20) There is nothing that sin did to the human nature that God is not able to undo. God is never concerned about a person's past, because grace is able to take the "vilest sinner" and make him whole. Grace is adequate to enable us to perform every action to which God directs us.

Nicolas lived up to his name and leaves of legacy for us of "victory over sin" and unselfish service to others.

What's In a Name: Nicodemus
John 3:1

Of the many encounters which Jesus had, the one with Nicodemus was special. Had he been a typical Pharisee, he would have been too proud to even consider coming to Christ to ask for spiritual insights. He was still governed by some peer pressure because he sought Jesus out at night so he would not be so visible. Yet he was driven to get answers for his own inquisitive mind.

Most of his contemporaries rejected Jesus as just another self-serving self-proclaimed messiah. But Nicodemus had investigated for himself and expressed his belief, "Rabbi, we know that You have come from God as a teacher." (Jn 3:2) The teachings had been attested to by the miracles and he needed to reconcile his beliefs with the growing awareness of the reality of the true Messiah.

Nicodemus centered in on the "how" questions. "How can a man be born when he is old?" (3:4) "How can these things be?" (3:9) Jesus took the time for His explanations to sink in. One of the most significant verses in the gospels (Jn 3:16) is given in response to Nicodemus' questions.

The name Nicodemus means "victorious among the people." One essential element of victory is perseverance and he certainly displayed that. The connotation of "victory" is not on the results, but on the means of success. God is always concerned about our processes, as much as our results. Most are familiar with the brand Nike which is a transliteration of the Greek word for victory. "Nike" implies both skill and perseverance in order to make a conquest.

Conquests, success, and victory are held up as the ideal of the American dream. But it's a fleeting notion. The thrill is momentary and then one must strike out after the next goal. Along the way, the process is always sacrificed on the altar of accomplishment. The politicians, bureaucrats, and business people have subscribed to the philosophy of the "ends justify the means." Sadly, even church leaders have followed that view, but God is never pleased.

Perhaps that is why Nicodemus is contrasted with other Jewish leaders of his day. When many of those leaders were prejudiced against Jesus and were trying to short-circuit a just process, Nicodemus raised the caution, "Does our law judge any man before it hears him, and knows what he does?" (Jn 7:51) That prejudice caused others to skew their view of him when he called for justice and many times it does the same today. Even when people have God-inspired visions, the temptation is so strong as to bypass challenges to get to the finish line. But God is more concerned with our character development than our conquests. To be "victorious among the people" it is essential to maintain strong relationships. It's hard for some personality types to remember that "people" is the business of the gospel. Even though God was "right" He initiated the reconciliation to mankind.

To build and heal people is much harder work than it is to complete a task. That is the only kind of victory that Calvary values. The "winners' crown" in heaven is filled with the trophies of redeeming grace.

Victory is listed by the "who" items, not the what or how!

What's In a Name: Noah
Genesis 6:8

Listen to too much news in your spirit will become agitated. Even though there were no modern media channels, in just a few generations, news of wickedness of man was overwhelming. "The Lord saw that the wickedness of man was great on the Earth, and that every intent of the thoughts of his heart was only evil continually." (Gen 6:5) No words would have to be changed to make that the headlines in 2010!

One of the consequences of sin is unrest. Send always disturbs the mind, the affections, and the spirit. It disturbs the mind because our thoughts are conflicted; we are forced to contend with the tension or try to block out sound reasoning. Sin agitates our affections because they are pulled away from moral goodness. Sin upsets our spirit because guilt settles in and we are pricked by our conscience. The greater the sin, the greater the unrest. It seems our world is encased with sin because there is unrest in every part of it.

It was in this morally corrupt world but "Noah found favor in the eyes of the Lord." (Gen 6:8) The greater the contrast, the easier something should be to spot. And Noah "stuck out" because his whole nature was different than his surroundings. Noah's name means rest. Rest in the topsy-turvy world would represent a sought after haven. Rest is not an isolated quality; it cannot be achieved without attachment of other developments.

"Noah was a righteous man" (6:9), i.e., his actions mimicked those of God. Righteousness always implies doing what is right. He is also described as "blameless in his generation," which speaks to the issue of integrity. Integrity is the congruency of motive, speech, and action. WYSIWYG! (What You See Is What You Get.) "Noah walked with God." In spite of the conflicts of his generation, Noah was at peace with himself, his neighbors, and God. That was a monumental achievement, and he lived up to his name.

When someone is in turmoil, it usually consumes all their time. Even if it doesn't, it still saps enough vitality away so that one cannot achieve his/her best. God had a huge assignment, and only Noah was available. Noah's heart of rest was essential for this task because he had to listen to the taunts of his friends and neighbors for 120 years while he built the ark. A person with a disturbed spirit could not keep focused long enough to complete the project.

Noah represented a type of Christ, who proclaimed, "come to me and I will give you rest." (Mt 11:28) The declaration, "There remains therefore a Sabbath rest for the people of God" (Heb 4:9) is clear that God's intention is for Christians to be at rest even in a flood of overwhelming circumstances. Noah had to remain at rest even when it looked like he was unsuccessful: "a few, that is, eight persons were brought safely through the water." (1 Peter 3:20) You don't have to walk many miles on this Earth to encounter troubled souls. Hebrews highlights the reason Noah was able to be at rest during the century plus leading up to the deluge and that was equated as faith. Often we are looking for something miraculous from God, when His instructions often come in the ordinary processes of life!

Faith, being the unseen, can be so dynamic that in the face of universal wickedness it becomes the anchor of rest for the soul.

What's In a Name: Onesimus
Philemon 10

As an apostolic missionary, Paul had occasion to touch lives all over the Mediterranean world. Paul rarely spent more than a few months in any given town. He would establish a church with the new converts, appoint leaders, and move on. His travels were periodically interrupted by times of imprisonment. While we do not have detailed accounts of his incarcerations, we do know that Paul continued to "do the work of the ministry" even while confined. During those periods Paul was dependent on God bringing to him those with whom He wanted Paul to intersect.

There was a slave named Onesimus who belonged to a man in Colosse in Asia Minor named Philemon. Philemon has responded to the gospel and developed a close relationship with Paul. Whether Paul was acquainted with Onesimus while he was with Philemon, we are not told. There must have been some significant conflict between master and slave for Onesimus to escape. Wherever else his wanderings, Onesimus ended up in Rome where Paul was being held.

Paul was very learned in Jewish law and knew the "fugitive statute," Deut 23:15-16. "You shall not hand over to his master a slave who has escaped from his master to you. He shall live with you in your midst, in the place which he shall choose in one of your towns where it pleases him; you shall not mistreat him." So Paul gave shelter to Onesimus, and did not notify Philemon that he had arrived.

The name Onesimus means "useful or profitable." There was probably great hope by his parents that Onesimus would mature into a useful person. Given his life with Philemon, it is quite obvious that he did not live up to his name. We're not quite sure how, but Onesimus seems to have "run up a bill," and somehow owed his master money. Under the influence of Paul, Onesimus began to change his habits and his attitudes. Instead of being a consumer he becomes a contributor. Finally, the day came when Paul felt it appropriate to send him back to Colosse.

Paul wrote a personal letter to Philemon and in it acknowledged Onesimus' past failures, calling him "useless" regarding his past. (v 11) But Paul refers to him as "my child, whom I have begotten in my imprisonment." (v 10) It focuses on the power of a re-birth. A genuine new birth sets the stage for reconciliation. In sending him back, Paul wants Philemon to accept him as a beloved brother, because I am "sending my very heart." (v 12) Redemption always provides a second chance.

Paul acknowledges the debt of Onesimus by assuming it himself. This offer to repay or make restitution is often a forgotten part of the conversion experience. (v 18-19) (See Ex 22:3-12) People who make their restitutions rarely return to those habits of sin. God understands human nature more than we acknowledge. Philemon no doubt had tried to reform his slave, and it never seemed to work. Human effort, by itself, is insufficient to effect a radical change of heart. But what is useless in the hands of man can become quite useful through the power of grace.

Christ Jesus can redeem all things and Onesimus is a clear illustration of grace taking someone we regard as worthless and making him "profitable" to the Kingdom!

What's In a Name: Saul to Paul
Acts 13:9

After the Gospels, there is no more familiar name in the New Testament than Paul. Even in the Acts of the Apostles, Paul dominates the scene from the time of his conversion on the Damascus Road in chapter nine. He is credited with authoring 13 or 14 of the 27 books in the New Testament.

Saul started out on a path diametrically opposed to Christianity. Born into a Pharisee family, he was energized by the legalism and leadership of that sect. Obtaining a great education, he prepared himself for dominance in the Jewish government. He learned "at the feet of Gamaliel, taught according to the strictness of our fathers' law, and was zealous toward God as you all are today."
(Acts 22:3 NKJV) He obviously had political connections and was able to obtain authority to harass and imprison Christians. "I journeyed to Damascus with authority and commission from the chief priests...." (Acts 26:12 NKJV)

The name Saul is an old Hebrew name meaning "asked or requested" but the implication is that it was a stern inquiry that demanded an answer. Saul was certainly true to his name at this stage in his life. He seemed to let no obstacle keep him from accomplishing his mission to destroy Christ followers and stamp out what he regarded as a "rogue religion."

Most Christians of that day were afraid to confront him, and I doubt if there would be any greater response from today's disciples. It may not have even occurred to anyone at that time to pray for the salvation of this "enemy number one." Too often we adopt the same stance and our limited faith doesn't even dream of converting those most opposed to us and our Christ.

But God had other plans and personally arrested Saul in a dramatic scene while he was pursuing his next victims. The scripture only records a brief conversation between Saul and God, but the revelation was sufficient to turn Saul 180 degrees and make a life-long commitment to Jesus. Once having made that U-turn, his old name just didn't fit.

Changing from Saul to Paul seemed a simple substitution of a "P" for an "S." But the results were emphatic. The name Paul means "stop, or come to an end." His new name signified not only that his old life had come to a complete stop, but that he had resigned from his own goals and ideals. Once again Paul lived up to his name.

We have no record of a formal "name change" or any ceremony signifying such. It was simply that the new name fit the new character God had infused. Too many professed Christians of today have little transformation from their old life. But Paul's life demonstrated what he wrote to the church at Corinth. "Therefore, if anyone is in Christ, he is a new creation; old things have passed away; behold, all things have become new." (2 Cor 5:17 NKJV)

The church as well as the whole has been blessed because the change of Saul to Paul. Perhaps we should identify the enemies of the gospel and pray they become the champions of Jesus.

Is your name still the same as it was BC? (Before Christ)

What's In a Name: Rahab
Joshua 2:1

The Bible has a singular theme of redemption. Beginning with Adam and Eve in Genesis, the story isn't primarily about creation and the origin of mankind. That is covered in just a few verses. By chapter three we're given details of man's sin and the punishment, but more importantly the promise of redemption. (Gen 3:15) Throughout the narratives of the various lives, time and time again redemption is given to those who will accept it. In Israel's history, Joshua assumed leadership just as they were ready to enter the Promised Land.

As a strategic military move, Joshua sent two spies to Jericho to get the lay of the land. Representing a people under covenant to be righteous, the record tells us "they went and came into the house of a harlot whose name was Rahab, and lodged there." (Josh 2:1) The scripture reports this sequence without an emotional reaction. Can you imagine the gasps in the audience if the spies were giving their report and said they had gone immediately to a harlot's house to spend the night?

The name Rahab means "proud." Whether her parents were proud to have this girl (which would be counter-cultural) or they wanted her to be proud, we are not told. But it appears Rahab may have been the most well-known prostitute in the city and was "proud" of the fact. Being a member of the "world's oldest occupation," she was also unholy in her name. God has little concern with what we've been.

It's at a divine intersection in life, when personal choices can determine the destiny that life hangs in the balance. The right choice to follow God in obedience changes everything. It is noted by James, "And in the same way was not Rahab the harlot also justified by works, when she received the messengers and sent them out by another way?" (Jam 2:25)

While God did not effect a name change, there was a radical transformation in character! She made a deal with the spies and upheld her end of the bargain. When the conquest of Jericho was in process, Joshua instructed the spies to extract Rahab and all those in her house as per the agreement. While the biblical narrative does not give us details, Rahab attracted the attention of Salmon and they married. As a result, Rahab became the great-grandmother of King David. (Mt 1:5-6) I'm amazed at how the Bible gives us scant details with major implications. Transformed from the town harlot to a spiritual matriarch, she in inserted into the lineage of Jesus Christ by God's redemptive power.

We see the extent of Ms. Proud becoming a woman of faith by her inclusion in the Hall of Faith. She and Sarah are the only two females mentioned by name in Hebrews 11. "By faith Rahab the harlot did not perish along with those who were disobedient, after she had welcomed the spies in peace." (Heb 11:31) Only God could write a script like this.

Our society doesn't believe that people can really be transformed, and they can't be apart from the grace of God. There have been numerous failures in the church as well. But these "trophies of redeeming grace" are magnificent enough to keep me evangelizing. The blood will never lose its power to turn pride into humility or sin to holiness.

The grace billboard along the highway simply reads "Rahab."

What's In a Name: Ruth
Ruth 1:4

The Old Testament book of Ruth is a dynamic story of both heartbreak and redemption. The story begins with a Jewish couple, Elimilech and Naomi, who move from Bethlehem to the country of Moab because there was a severe famine in Israel at the time. One of the challenges of living in a place where there are different cultures has to do with children. Generally, children do not have the biases of their parents, nor the difficulty with culture issues such as customs or language. The boys in the story, Mahlon and Chilion, were attracted to the girls in the area and each married.

Tragedy struck and Elimilech, Mahlon and Chilion all died within a short period of time. Eventually, Naomi decided to return back home to the Bethlehem area. In so doing, she encouraged her daughters-in-law to go back to their families as well. Orpah consented and returned, but Ruth insisted that she stay with Naomi in spite of all the arguments put forth.

The history of the Moabites is interesting. Occupying territory on the southeastern border of the Dead Sea, they had their beginning from a man named Moab. Moab was the product of incest from Lot with his older daughter. That nefarious beginning was compounded by Moab's refusal to let Israel pass through its border en route to the Promise Land after the Exodus. Because of this historical denial of entry, an instruction was given, "An Ammonite or Moabite shall not enter the assembly of the LORD; even to the tenth generation none of his descendants shall enter the assembly of the LORD forever." (Deut 23:3 NKJV)

The Jewish mindset was that Moabites were unfit for any kind of association, much less friendship. Our bent toward stereotyping is so strong that we fail to recognize the power of God's grace in redemption. Naomi was surprised when Ruth's loyalty to her (a mother-in-law) was stronger than other family ties, her religious upbringing, as well as other cultural issues. Ironically, Ruth was simply living out her name, which means "friend or close associate." We are all too familiar with friendships (or the lack thereof) in our society. It has been stated that rarely does a person make more than two true friends in their entire life.

But Ruth was not to be deterred from her attachment to Naomi, even though no promises of any favorable future were presented. The unfolding of God's redemptive power in the subsequent events in Bethlehem is astounding. Boaz, a leader in Israel, was attracted to this young lady because of her character. He moved into the role of "redeemer," a term with special meaning in Jewish society, and thus became the husband of this Moabitess.

Go to Matthew chapter one and you will find the name of several women, Ruth being one of them. Ruth became the daughter-in-law of Rahab and thus both were in the lineage of Jesus. What the world despises and rejects becomes the object of redemption. God delights in showing the power of transforming grace is always greater than the greatest damage that sin is able to do.

Ruth, a true friend, is a shining example of the transforming power of God's grace, no matter what our origins or culture!

What's In a Name: Samson
Judges 13:24

In the years following the death of Joshua, Israel became a disorganized confederacy of the twelve tribes. Following the seventy some years of strong leadership, no national leader was designated. That fostered a time of spiritual confusion, and the nation succumbed to idolatry, pagan intermarriage, foreign political domination, and other major sins. When their foreign captors became oppressive, the people would cry out to God and God would raise up a deliverer. Freed from their slavery, the people would serve God while that leader lived. Following the death of the judge, the people would again slip into sin and subsequently into slavery.

Following the death of Abdon, the 12th judge, "the sons of Israel again did evil in the sight of God." (Jud 13:1) and they became subject to the Philistines. During this time God visited a man and wife and commissioned them to produce the next deliverer. As a part of that assignment, the boy baby was to be a Nazarite from birth which required that he have no alcoholic drinks, no unclean food, and no cutting of his hair. Usually the Nazarite vow was for a short period of time, but this son was to be a Nazarite "from the womb to the tomb." (See Jud 13:7)

When the promised son was born, his mother named him Samson. Not having been given a name in the assignment, "Samson" seemed appropriate because it means "sunlight" or 'sunshine!" Sin and captivity always produce darkness in people's souls. Babies by their very nature provide a "spark of life" or a ray of sunshine. As for Samson, he was a bright light, someone born to be a "deliverer and leader of his people. Had I asked in the beginning what you thought the name meant, most would have guessed "strength." His strength was legendary and often he would be accosted by his enemies, the Philistines. Usually single-handedly he would defeat the Philistines and cause them much grief, though it took a while for complete deliverance.

It quickly became apparent that "sunlight" had some serious shadows. His weakness for women became an Achilles heel. Samson had some great exploits: killing a thousand men with a donkey jawbone as his only weapon, killing a young lion with his bare hands. In the end, the harlot Delilah coaxed his secrets from him. Samson's source of sunlight had been extinguished and hope for real deliverance took a nose dive. Samson's actions confirm a universal truth: You can conquer the world, but if you don't conquer yourself, you still lose in the end. Spiritual losses are not final unless you shut off God's proffered help. Samson, like a lot of people, turned to God as he labored in prison. "Then Samson called to the Lord and said…'please remember me and please strengthen me.'" (Jud 16:28) The prayer was coming from a repentant heart and even with all his failures, Samson used his recovering faith to discover God's forgiveness. Heavenly sunlight broke through those prison bars and warmed his soul.

Of the thirteen judges of that period, Samson had the most failure. But God's plan of redemption is so great that Samson is the only one of those judges to be mentioned by name in the "hall of faith." (Heb 11:32)

The sunlight may have been obscured for a time, but God specializes in writing the last chapters of people's lives through faith!

What's In a Name: Samuel
1 Samuel 1:20

Hannah was a lady with mixed emotions. On one hand she was the dearly beloved wife of Elkanah, but she had not children. To make matters worse, the other wife is termed a "rival" who would "provoke her bitterly to irritate her because the Lord had closed her womb." (1 Sam 1:5-6) The family made a yearly pilgrimage to the house of the Lord. Peninnah, the other wife, would use the occasion to goad Hannah even more. (v 7) Elkanah meant well when he told Hannah, "Am I not better to you than ten sons?" (v 8) But his comment did little to assuage the pain in her heart.

So Hannah cried out to God. "She, greatly distressed, prayed to the Lord, and wept bitterly." (v 10) Her grief was so deep that she mouthed her prayer, but nothing was audible. Eli, the priest, accused her of drunkenness. She explained she was "oppressed in spirit" and was simply pouring out her heart to God. (v 15) For men, we struggle to read a woman's unspoken thoughts, but God is a master at hearing her heart. Moved by her desire, God allowed her to conceive. Even though she made promises to God regarding this son, God did not require anything from her.

When her son was born, she named him Samuel, which means "heard by God." Many people offer prayer, but it's getting our prayers heard and answered that makes the difference. Even though the name Hannah means favored (by God), there was just a slight delay in the fulfillment of that favor. In keeping with her vow, she gave Samuel back to God "for as long as he lives." (v 28) Early on in his time at Shiloh, God called out to Samuel. At first, not recognizing the voice of God, by the third call Samuel responded with "I'm listening." With a heritage set by his mother's prayers, and cemented with personal conversation with God, Samuel's life was fairly well defined. Following the death of Eli, Samuel was thrust into leading the whole nation. God opened the door to Samuel's style of leadership. "The Lord appeared again at Shiloh, because the Lord revealed Himself to Samuel at Shiloh by the word of the Lord." (3:21)

Samuel's ministry was centered around conversations with God. His mother's words were his direction and inspiration: "The Lord has given me my petition which I asked of Him." (1:27) God often lavishes His favor, so Hannah ended up with three more sons and two daughters. (2:21) At each juncture of his ministry, Samuel called on God. When pressed to appoint a king, "Samuel prayed to the Lord." (8:6) When he had admonished Saul, "Samuel was distressed and cried out to the Lord all night." (15:11)

From the creation of man, it appears God delighted in conversation with mankind. The interaction isn't an end in itself. God thrills to act on our requests when they are in accordance with His will. Samuel had established an altar at this home in Ramah. It shows his dedication to prayer, instilled in him by his mother's example. (See 1 Sam 7:17)

All sorts of religions have prayers as a part of their practices. Truthfully, few people care that we pray. Changing the world comes when we are "heard of God."

Do you get your prayers answered? "The effectual fervent prayer of a righteous man avails (accomplishes) much." (Jam 5:16)

What's In a Name: Sarah
Genesis 17:15

When we are first introduced to Abraham in the Bible, it quickly mentions the name of his wife, Sarai. (Gen 11:29) This was quite unusual as women were not often listed by name in ancient records. The name means "the head person, or dominative one". In the vernacular, we may have called her "bossy." But the first distinguishing comment about her is that "she had no child." (v 30)

Again, I cannot imagine what would motivate parents to name their child "bossy," which we usually reserve for a cow, and only after we had observed them. Whether prophetic or not, those tendencies are clearly seen in her domination over her maid, Hagar. Sarai was apparently a real "looker," and with an "attitude" that made her attractive to certain elements. Sarai was taken into custody by Pharaoh who intended to add her to his harem until God intervened. (12:14-17)

God's promise to Abram that he would have a son was also a personal promise to Sarai. It was not to be just of Abraham, for he eventually had eight sons. There was to be only one "son of promise" and that was to be born to Sarai. And just as God changed Abram to Abraham, God changed Sarai to Sarah, (17:15) "Sarah shall be her name." This indicated a shift both in role and in character. Sarah means, princess, daughter of a Sovereign. While Sarai assumed authority over others, Sarah had power now because of who she had become.

The crowning virtue of a woman in those days was to mother a son. And in this case it was designed for her to mother royalty. "And I will bless her, and indeed I will give you a son by her.

Then I will bless her, and she shall be a mother of nations; kings of peoples shall come from her." (17:16) Her designation as a princess came from the Sovereign of the Universe. And her destiny included descendants who would be kings. Even she did not understand that this new royal line would include Jesus, a savior for all men, and our coming King.

Sarah no longer had to insist on her limited authority, but could with confidence display the authority of her Father. It is noteworthy that she is one of only two women mentioned by name in the "hall of faith" in Hebrews 11. "By faith even Sarah herself received ability to conceive even beyond the proper time of life, since she considered Him faithful who had promised." (v 11)

Sarah was not riding the coattails of her husband in the faith department. Her personal faith was just as strong and vibrant, and her participation in the realization of the promise (nine months plus) was infinitely more than Abrahams'. While other's faith can be helpful and encouraging to us in difficult times, we must find our own personal faith. God wants a direct relationship with each of us.

When God changes someone's name, it's for a good reason. And Sarah is the only such woman mentioned in scripture for this honor. God's design for her new role, and the transforming change in character were significant enough that a new name was warranted. Perhaps if your name was "bossy" you'd want a new name too. But God doesn't have a superficial department that changes labels on a whim.

When He finds people who "consider Him faithful," He initiates eternal changes. What will your new name be?

What's In a Name: Simon Peter
Matthew 4:18

The most visible of all the apostles was Simon Peter. A successful fisherman from the Galilee area, he and his brother Andrew were the first recorded disciples of Jesus. Only the Gospel of John records the account of Andrew, initially a disciple of John the Baptist, who on the day following the baptism of Jesus told him that Jesus was the Messiah. Andrew made the decision to become a disciple of Jesus Christ, but immediately recruited his brother Simon. (See John 1:40-42)

The name Simon means to "hear intelligently." While Simon's personality is presented as bombastic, it is clear that Simon did listen to his brother. We live in a culture where listening is mostly a lost art. And listening "intelligently" is extremely rare. Our basic pride hinders our ability to listen, and distractions and dullness contribute to our poor hearing functions. Good listening skills must be developed through strong determination.

Simon quickly became the natural "leader" among the twelve disciples. Perhaps it was because he was not afraid to speak out at every occasion. He witnessed firsthand many extraordinary events such as the transfiguration of Christ and was the only disciple to walk on water. He allowed Jesus to change him from a fisherman to a fisher of men.

Simon apparently had a nickname, Peter. When and how that was given, we can only guess. Somewhere along the way, Jesus focused on the nickname Peter. Peter means "a large rock." Simon Peter was initially anything but a "rock." Bombastic and volatile, he was always stretching the limits.

In a meeting with the disciples, Jesus questioned them concerning who other Jews believed him to be. Peter comes forth with the Great Confession, "You are the Christ." (Mt 16:16 NKJV) Peter obviously had been listening intelligently. But Jesus explained another dimension for calling him Peter. He had received direct "revelation" from God the father. (16:18) Spiritual truths cannot be learned by mere education alone. They are revealed from the Spirit of God to our spirit intuitively.

The world culture is one of pluralism. With all the swirling theologies and philosophies, it is essential that we find an anchor, or "rock" of belief. Israel was one of the few monotheistic societies of its day. Perhaps that is why Jesus was so emphatic about Peter's confession. While Peter had a major failure in his betrayal of Christ, his repentance was genuine and he once again regained a fresh revelation of Christ. That enabled him to receive the Holy Spirit on the day of Pentecost.

He was able to fulfill the prophecy given by Joel ("this is that" Acts 2:16-21, Joel 2:28,32) and his message that day produced 3000 converts. Now that's a real rock!

What's in a Name: Solomon
2 Samuel 12:24

When David ascended to the throne of Israel, there were still many areas of Canaan that had not been conquered. From the time that he killed Goliath, he was well-known for his military prowess. He led is a rogue army in many battles, and returned victorious. It always seemed ironic to me that the object of war was to gain peace. Peace was David's goal, but it eluded him his whole life. Militarily, David could probably have achieved his goal but personal failures doomed them. Following his adulterous affair and subsequent involvement with the murder of Uriah, Nathan, the prophet, informed him. "Now, therefore, the sword will never depart from your house." (2 Sam 12:10)

Even though God granted David forgiveness, the consequences of sin loomed large. In addition to perpetual war, the son from the affair died. (2 Sam 12:18). None of this deterred David from seeking peace for the country. In the aftermath of these events, God showed the power of his redemption. To David and Bathsheba was born a second son, this one from a union of love, not lust. As parents are prone to do, they wish in their children what they themselves fail to achieve, and they named the son, Solomon. Solomon is a variation on the Hebrew greeting of shalom, and also means peace or peaceful. (2 Sam 12:24) There is an expression regarding Solomon that is not repeated anywhere in Scripture and that is "now the Lord loved him." We know that God loves us all but there seemed to be a special attachment to Solomon.

Later, Solomon through right choices was endowed with great wisdom. It's another case of a man defining his name. To us Solomon means wisdom, but his parents wanted peace. God granted both. "A son shall be born to you who shall be a man of rest, and I will give him rest from all his enemies on every side, for his name shall be Solomon (peaceful) and I will give peace and quiet to Israel in his days." (1 Chr 22:9) Because of his father's preparation, Solomon was able to have a peaceful life.

Solomon was not the name that God had chosen for him. The Lord "sent words through Nathan the prophet, and he named him Jedediah for the Lord sake." (2 Sam 12:25) Jedediah means "beloved of the Lord." While it is significant that God would send name for this son, there is no record that the name was accepted or ever used again.

Peace is often an elusive goal. One is not peaceful simply because circumstances are congruent with our wishes. Peace must begin within a person. Peace is the lack of disturbance or conflict and cannot be achieved without harmony with God.

Peace implies a sense of security and order. Peace is not a commodity that one can acquire; it is achieved when things that agitate us are quieted. Even though Solomon had peace as a nation ("so Judah and Israel lived in safety, every man under his vine and his fig tree from Dan to Beersheba all the days of Solomon." 1 Kings 4:25), Solomon allowed all sorts of sins to be introduced into his life, primarily through his 700 wives. Those sins not only caused personal peace to evaporate, he became a cynical man in his later years. His fame, his wealth, and his wisdom were squandered; his peace was gone in the end and the next generation began a new round of conflict.

What a difference he could have made just to live up to his name of peace!

What's In a Name: Stephen
Acts 6:5

While there are longer stories in the scripture, one of the very compelling accounts of martyrdom is one of Stephen. How long Stephen was a part of the followers of Christ we are not told. But when a need arose in the early church regarding caring for the Hellenistic Jewish widows, the decision was made to appoint deacons to provide that service. The early church leaders did not select these men based on their experience of serving food. (See Acts 6:1,2) The implication is that the group was given the assignment of selecting the deacons based on qualifications iterated by the twelve apostles. "Select from among you, brethren, seven men of good reputation, full of the Spirit and of wisdom, whom we may put in charge of this task." (Act 6:3)

Anytime a statement finds "approval with the whole congregation" (v 5) we can be confident that God is guiding those leaders. "<u>They</u> chose Stephen, a man full of faith and of the Holy Spirit." (v 5) Choosing someone for office should first of all be based on Christian character. If the church could learn this basic lesson, we would save ourselves a lot of problems that we subsequently encounter.

The name Stephen means "entwined as in making a wreath" and the implication is that wreaths were made to give honor. Wreaths were presented in a public ceremony usually to honor someone who had privately carried out a noble deed. While the scripture does not detail for us the work of serving tables for which the office of deacon was designated, it seems certain that Stephen and the others carried out their assignment with both competence and passion. No grumbling is ever mentioned again in the New Testament by these widows or their advocates. In the carrying out of the assignment, these men saw the greater vision that this was ministry as much as the apostles' work. For this period of time, it was having a greater impact. "And Stephen, full of grace and power, was performing great wonders and miracles among the people." (Act 6:8) Any act of service, however lowly, can be the foundation for incredible acts of God!

Whenever we are doing great things for God, you can be sure there will be a backlash. Even though religious leaders tried to argue with Stephen in public, "they were unable to cope with the wisdom and the Spirit with which he was speaking." (v 10) These men turned to legal processes and had him arrested. Unable to respond to his legal arguments, they simply rallied the "jury" (Sanhedrin) and condemned him to death. Oppressive governments, including ours, still follow the same tactics today.

Even though they were able to stoned Stephen to death using their illegal processes, the whole story shows the irony God implants in disasters. Saul (Paul) was moved by the experience and later became an effective missionary. The church was persecuted so that it scattered over the whole area and both Gentiles and Jews were evangelized. In recognition of Stephen's martyrdom, (and indicative of his name) Jesus welcomed him into heaven. Even though Jesus sat down on the right hand of the Father, in this case He stood to honor this saint of God.

It may later be revealed to us what was entwined in the victory wreath presented to Stephen. Perhaps it was his crown, hand-made by Christ!

What's In a Name: Timothy
1 Timothy 1:2

Whenever we hear of someone who has had or is having an impact in the church or the world, we are interested to know how that person came into his/her position of influence. If, as John Maxwell declares, leadership is influence, we should be able to evaluate leadership potential by influence. Who are the ones who influenced this person's life, and subsequently who are they influencing.

The story of Timothy in the scriptures is an excellent example of influence. For whatever reason, Timothy's father, a Greek, seems to be absent from the development of his son's life. But in the second letter by Paul, mention is made of the impact by Timothy's mother, Eunice, and his grandmother, Lois. Timothy seems to be an only son, and his mother and grandmother devote their life to rearing a godly young man. Paul writes, "greatly desiring to see you, being mindful of your tears, that I may be filled with joy, when I call to remembrance the genuine faith that is in you, which dwelt first in your grandmother Lois and your mother Eunice, and I am persuaded is in you also." 2 Tim 1:4-5 NKJV

From this passage we can conclude several things:
1. Tthat there was a strong bond between Paul and Timothy as evidenced by the young man's tears.
2. Tthat both Eunice and Lois were women of genuine faith
3. That these ladies not only recognized the importance of passing on a legacy, but understood the need to impart that faith in Timothy.

Seeing a subsequent generation not only exhibit the "faith of the fathers" but also demonstrate they possess faith in a direct relationship to God is not easy to achieve. In addition to the direct line of descent, these ladies thrust Timothy into the arena of Paul's influence.

Not a strong person physically, Timothy needed medical care but also seemed to need development in character and ministry. Paul was able to add value to his life during the traveling days in missionary work. With each of these three influencers in Timothy's life, they were able to communicate the message of his name: "dear to God."

Psychologists of today are fond of talking about self-image, but one of the best antidote to a fractured ego is to know who values you. If someone we admire values us, it bolsters our spirit to the point that we can handle a lot of criticism. When it is the Supreme Being of the Universe who considers us valuable, we can be on top of the world.

One thing in which our generations have been very weak over the past century is the ability to pass on our faith. That transference of godly character can rarely developed by condemnation and abrasiveness. In contrast, knowing how dear we are, i.e., unconditionally loved, is so transforming that the recipients of such love tend to exceed all expectations for them. Who would have thought that this "weakling half-breed" would later be commissioned as a bishop in the early church and history records a successful tenure?

How many "sons in the faith" do you have? You can have many if you treat them as "Timothy's." To the degree that you convey to them how dear they are to God, and to yourself, you put yourself into position to propagate a living faith in and through the next generation!

What's In a Name: Zechariah
Zechariah 1:1

The prophet Jeremiah had been give the assignment of delivering the bad news to the Israelites: "Because of your sin, you will go into captivity for seventy years." And it wasn't just the length of time; they would be in bondage to Babylon, an evil empire. The first deportation occurred in 606 BC. Babylon was so wicked that it too fell in 539 BC—just 67 years later. The Persian kings who conquered Babylon, by comparison, were benevolent and instituted a policy of sending ethnic groups back to their homelands. So three years after the Persian rule began, the Jews started returning to Jerusalem. (See the historical notations in 2 Chronicles 36:20-23.)

It is in this post-captivity period that Zechariah ministered. The walls of the city were rebuilt under Nehemiah's leadership and work on the temple foundation began. Local opposition was so fierce that progress on the temple was halted for 16 years. Through the preaching of Zechariah and contemporary Haggai, the people responded to God. The name Zechariah means, "God has remembered." The people were convinced that God was remembering and they quickly engaged in the work. It still took another five years to complete the restoration.

As with many of the Old Testament prophets, their words fulfilled a dual role. They spoke of both the present and the future. The hope of salvation in the Hebrew mindset was connected to the actual existence of the temple. God had indicated that the Shekinah, the visible "presence" of the Almighty would dwell above the mercy seat and between the cherubim. To see both Jerusalem and the temple restored was a fulfillment that God had remembered His covenant!

The tabernacle/temple was always meant to be symbolic of the unfolding of God's ultimate plan of redemption.

There are seven messianic promises in Zechariah which are identified in the New Testament. The first relates to God dwelling in our midst (Zech 2:10-13 v Rev 5:13; 6:9; 21:24; 22:1-5) as the Lamb on the Throne. Another relates to the holy priesthood. (Zech 3:8 v. Jn 2:19-21; Eph 2:20-21; 1 Pet 2:5) Zechariah clearly saw Jesus as a heavenly high priest. (Zec 6:12-13 v Heb 4:4; 8:12)

The triumphal entry was envisioned by Zechariah (9:9-10 v Mt 21:4-5; Mk 11:9-10; Jn 12:13-15) Matthew records the price for which Jesus was sold, thirty pieces of silver, and the money, when it was returned by Judas, bought the bought the potter's field. (See Zech 11:12-13 v Mt 26:14-15; 27:9) The gospel writer John refers to the piercing of Jesus body. (Zech 12:10 v Jn 19:34, 37) The final Messianic prophecy by Zechariah regarded the sheep scattering when the shepherd was smitten (Zec 13:1, 6-7) and was referenced by Matthew (26:31) and John (16:32)

Life cycles through both blessings and disappointments. God has made incredible promises to His people, but in the middle of life's crises they often fade into the background. Through those seventy years many Jews no doubt wondered if there would ever be an end to their sorrow. The young may have heard their parents talk about the promise. But God's memory is perfect and timely. We may need a few more Zechariahs to remind us: God has never forgotten a promise, a covenant, or an oath.

Faithful prophets like Zechariah are there to remind us that God's clocks keep perfect time!

About the Author

A fifth consecutive generation minister, Bob Bedford has served as pastor, regional superintendent, missionary and educator. He currently serves as director of the Global School of Theology, of the University of Science, Arts, and Technology. He has ministered all over the United States and many foreign countries. He previously pastored churches in Florida, Indiana, and Pennsylvania. He holds a Bachelor of Theology degree from Asbury Bible College and a Doctor of Religion from Indiana Christian University.

An avid reader of scripture, he has read the entire Bible through once a year for the past 55 years, a practice he continues. In this book, he shares insights into biblical names which will greatly enhance the reader's understanding of God's interaction with humanity.

He has been married to Linda for over forty-six years, and they are the parents of four daughters who have blessed them with eight grandchildren and a great-granddaughter. He and Linda reside in Seminole, Florida.

www.ingramcontent.com/pod-product-compliance
Lightning Source LLC
Chambersburg PA
CBHW071518040426
42444CB00008B/1705